POUNDS PINFOLDS OF CUMBRIA

POUNDS AND PINFOLDS OF CUMBRIA

"The History and Mystery of Pinfolds"

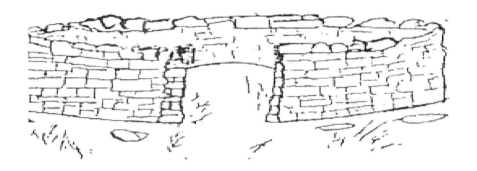

Nigel Mills

Preface.

This research is intended to be an informative and documented historical text and provide a look at the way of life of the people who built, maintained, managed and lived with the physical presence and function of the village pound or pinfold. It is written for the general reader and aims to encourage interest by local historians in these modest structures and hopefully help to halt their disappearance from our landscape.

A general definition is that:-

A pound or pinfold is a structure built to confine stray stock or any animal found grazing on land for which their owner did not have permission. Once confined a pinder, usually appointed by the manor court, was responsible for the care of the animals until the owner had paid the fine imposed by the court.

A typical pound or pinfold

Ask most people what they know about pounds and pinfolds and they will shake their heads and look blank. Many have not even noticed the small round or rectangular building at the edge of their village and if they have, they do not give it a second thought. This lack of awareness is why many pounds and pinfolds have disappeared from the landscape or remain only as piles of stones. Hopefully I can increase public knowledge and encourage preservation of pounds and pinfolds.

This research, carried out to satisfy my curious mind, has led me to many of the more remote villages and smaller towns in Cumbria and in doing so I have met many people who have helped me identify the locations and kindly given me access to their property to photograph and examine the pinfold. As well as spending many hours personally surfing the Internet I wish to thank the friends and family who have helped and supported me over the past few years. I also wish to thank the staff at the Cumbria Archive offices I have visited during this research and the Lorton & Derwent Fells Local History Society for their support in getting started. I hope that as a result of this work more people will visit these structures and respect and understand what they stood for in a time far removed from our present way of life.

My main focus is modern day Cumbria which includes the pre-1974 Counties of Westmorland, Cumberland, Lancashire North of the Sands (Furness and Cartmel Peninsula) and a part of West Yorkshire (Kirkby Lonsdale and Sedbergh). In the era of the pound and pinfold this area contained a mix of manors, townships, fells, commons and unenclosed waste. Animal husbandry methods, the general state of fencing and the lack of enclosure led to regular impounding of straying livestock. Although urban development has changed the landscape, the mainly rural environment of this area means that perhaps it has happened on a smaller scale than in many areas of England and as a result some fine examples of pounds and pinfolds still exist.

Our social and industrial heritage receives much attention, aimed it seems to me, especially at the grand, the romantic or the easily observable buildings of past ages. My aim here is to inform and create more interest in the pounds and pinfolds of Cumbria by explaining what they are, why they are there and what place they played in the life of our ancestors.

Acknowledgements

I would like to express my thanks to Friends of the Lake District, Prof. Angus Winchester and Derek Denman of Lorton & Derwent Fells Local History Society who in conjunction with Lancaster University gave me advice and encouragement to commence this project. Whitehaven Archive Service for access to archival material material and Lord Egremont for permission to reproduce material from the Leconfield Archive.

I am also very grateful to family and friends for their support and humorous encouragement over the past few years. A special thanks to John Wilkin and Stuart Harling for the early research in the wilds of Cumbria and a special thanks to Stuart who almost without question drove along some of the narrowest lane in Cumbria in search of the mysterious and often vanished pinfold.

YouCaxton Publications

24 High Street, Bishop's Castle, Shropshire. SY3 8JX
www.youCaxton.co.uk

©Photographs by Stuart Harling and Nigel Mills

ISBN 978-1-909644-45-8

Printed and bound in Great Britain.

Contents

Part I

An Introduction to Pounds and Pinfolds

Pound, Pinfold or Sheepfold?

Each pound or pinfold, although usually a simply built structure, has a character and history of its own and those that still remain stand proud though often neglected. A number are protected by the Listed Buildings and Conservation Act 1990[1] such as the pound at Field Broughton.

The use of the terms pound and pinfold can, but should not, cause confusion. In practice they mean the same and are therefore interchangeable. Whether a structure is referred to as a pound or pinfold seems quite arbitrary. I have analysed numerous maps and other reference documents believing that perhaps the use of the word pound or pinfold depended on a specific area or was a north v south or east v west practice but this appears not to be the case.

In many instances, but by no means all, the Ordnance Survey First Edition 1:2,500 and 1:560,000 scale maps show their location and names them as a pound or pinfold. When these maps were drawn up in the mid ninetenth century it is likely that the pound or pinfold had already been out of use for at least one generation so reliable oral evidence was unlikely to be available. Each surveyor was responsible for mapping large areas of Cumbria and I understand from Ordnance Survey (OS) that the surveyor might rely on local sources to identify a pound or pinfold and use the local name. He could also use his personal expertise and record what he considered to be the proper term according to his personal preference. Hence each site could either be recorded as a pound or a pinfold. In fact there are examples where the same fold is recorded alternately a pound and then a pinfold and vice versa on different revisions of the OS map.

References to pounds and pinfolds, earlier than the OS maps, are found in many sources including manorial court records, vestry records, parish council minutes and other archive documents. From the earliest records they have been known variously as Punfald, Pinfould, poundfold or

---

1   www.english-heritage

Pundfeld from which our modern terms of pound and pinfold are no doubt derived.

The Oxford English Dictionary(OED) gives the definitions of the terms pound and pinfold in various forms including punde, pownde, poundfold, and many other variations. It also suggests that in written Middle English there developed a confusion between the letters O and U and pound also came to mean a body of still water or pond. The English canal system uses the term pound for an area of water where barges are stored. Similarly the term pinfold has been written in various forms and has several derivations. The OED traces and gives examples of the use of these words to as early as 1170 with many examples of the use through the fourteenth and Fifteenth centuries.

The term used in the Manorial Records examined tended to be fold when referring to a pound and the earliest discovered formal reference I found refers to a breach of the fold referred to as a foldbreach as in this extract for 1473 in the records of Derwent Fells Capital Court.[2]

Capital Court of Derwentfett held on the eighth day of October in the 12ᵗʰ year of the reign of King Edward IV.

The Tenants   Allerdale.

Fines 8s 6d. Brakenthwayt presents John Strb for his servant for 1 foldbreach against John Thomlynson junior.

Lorton presents Peter Milner for fishing John Wilkynson for the same John Wilkynson of Lorton for shedding the blood of John son of Alan Williamson

In the 1649 Parliamentary Survey for the Manor of Lorton the term poundfold is used in describing the boundary of the township of Over Lorton with the Manor of Lorton. It reads:

"...and soe along Peals of the Tenters westwards to the poundfold and so over the beck...."

This refers to the poundfould at Lorton which was on the area of land situated adjacent to White Beck and overlooked by the famous Lorton Yew. Even though the pound has long since disappeared the small piece of land is still known locally as the poundfould.

---

2   WRO D/LEC 299 ROLL 8-10

In Cumbria most of the pinfolds that remain are built of locally sourced stone. In parts of England where forests were abundant, wood was used to construct the early pinfolds and provide fencing for the enclosure but these did not last and I have found no evidence of them in Cumbria. However, two examples of an early pinfold constructed of mixed hedging still exist. The first is a small area banked and hedged at Threapland and the second is a small grassed over and hedged outcrop of rock in the parish of Crosthwaite in the Lyth Valley used as a safe place for livestock to gather when the valley flooded. The latter is known as Pinfold Hill and thanks to its owner, the parish council, the hedging is being reinstated to its former glory.

Two typical examples of a more traditional pinfold are:

Field Broughton pound on White Moss Common just two miles north of Cartmel in the south of Cumbria. This is a circular pound owned by Broughton East Parish Council, Grade II listed and well maintained.

Hilton pinfold near Appleby in the north of Cumbria. This pound is rectangular at the edge of the village green.

Field Broughton Pound

Hilton Pinfold

These examples of are built of field and boulder stones and reflect the commonly available local stone at each location. Examples where a more refined design is used are at Kirkby Thore and Dalton-in-Furness which both use dressed limestone with ornamental triangular coping.

As described above, a pinfold is the term applied to the functional building used to impound stray animals under Manorial law and custom. Sheepfolds are different from and have a purpose distinct from that of a pinfold. They may, however, easily be confused visually, as their construction of dry stone walling is similar to that of some pinfolds in rural Cumbria[3].

---

3 CRO EM /5/1

The notable difference between the two is that sheepfolds are usually found on open fell or in field corners and are built to aid sheep management and provide shelter. There are several examples in my research where the original purpose of the structure named as a sheepfold on the OS map is ambiguous. Their location on open land would indicate a sheepfold but archive and OS references infer they may have been used as a pinfold in the rural fell side villages of Cumbria. When the commons were driven to collect illegally grazing stock any strays found would be confined in a pinfold but where these were not available a sheepfold would be used. Some of the larger ones became known as mountain pinfolds such as the one on Stockdale Moor. Not surprisingly there are examples of the Ordnance Survey classifying a structure as a sheepfold on one map and when later maps were prepared the same building becomes a pinfold and vice versa. At Bewaldeth the 1867 and 1886 OS maps show a "pinfold" but on the 1900 version it is called a "sheepfold". On the fell side near the village of Dent the OS map for 1853 shows a structure and names it as a pinfold but forty years later it is described as a sheepfold. This change is possibly because at the time of the revision or survey the function of the pinfold had long since become obsolete so it was described by its contemporary use. Conversely however the fold at Edenhall is shown on all maps as sheepfold but referred to officially by the parish council as a pinfold.

All Shapes and Sizes.

The pinfolds of Cumbria in our villages, towns and countryside appear in numerous different styles and sizes as well as using different building material but why? The reason for this variety can be surmised as follows. The poorer rural communities would have the available field and river boulders available and the skills to build their pinfold using tried and tested dry stone walling techniques, a skill used throughout Cumbria. These structures would be cheap to erect but would need constant repair. The more affluent townships could afford to use mortar and dressed limestone or sandstone to erect more substantial and robust pinfolds, especially if all or some of them were Manorial pounds and financed wholly or partly by the Lord of the Manor.

The building material used could well have influenced the shape of the fold with field stone lending itself more readily to a circular construction to avoid the weight stresses that come with squared off corners. However dressed and cut stone largely avoided this problem and with the use of mortar a substantial square or rectangular fold could be constructed.

Several other theories exist suggesting why they are a certain shape. A round or oval structure avoids the risk of smaller animals being trapped by larger ones in a corner and being suffocated or injured as result but it also makes the job of the pounder more difficult when catching a particularly lively animal as he could not "corner" it to catch it. In superstitious times it was believed that round enclosures such as a pinfold "leaves no corner for the devil to hide" and so this may have been an influence.

As well as the variations in the overall shape of the pinfold the size of them also differed. Originally the walls would have been between five to seven feet high both to keep the livestock in and to stop the animals being illegally "rescued" by their owners. Many surviving  examples have been repaired or rebuilt numerous times over their history. Many more have been robbed of stone and changed in shape, at Dearham by house building, at Culgaith (see image) by road widening or as at Great Asby just to tidy the boundary of the manor house.

The ground area inside the pinfold had to be large enough to cope with different sized livestock varying from geese and sheep through to cows and horses, and no doubt sometimes together. This led to pinfolds being constructed of various sizes depending on the type of animal it was expected to confine. A tether stone may have been used to ensure the larger animals were limited in their movement as is thought to be the case at Brampton, Appleby.

Location of Pinfolds.

At the time of its original build a typical pinfold location would be at the edge of a settlement or manor boundary, on waste or common land and close to a water source. Most villages and settlements would have built their own and also many would have a common and a manorial pound. As the waste and common land was enclosed a new pound was often established on a new site. A common pound would be one built and paid for by local yeoman, perhaps with some financial help from the lord or major landowner and it would be used to impound strays found within the township. A manorial pound would be one built by the lord of the manor and located at the manor boundary or near the manor house. This would be used to impound strays from a neighbouring manor or from outside the area.

In parts of Cumbria where there existed large swathes of common land the commons were regularly driven on instruction from the Lord and any livestock found grazing without explicit permission were enclosed in a manorial pound. These pounds were found at the edge of the common or waste or in a strategic position close to the droving roads. On agistment grounds large sheepfold structures, referred to as mountain pinfolds on the OS maps, were built such as the one on Stockdale Moor, Kinniside.

Another factor determining the location was the availability of a water source. The pinder would need to regularly water the impounded stock so a nearby well or stream was essential. Some pinfolds were actually built over a spring such as Penruddock pinfold. Crook pinfold channels spring water from the adjacent field to provide a continuous source of water and Kentmere pound encloses part of a small stream. Others such as Outgate pound are adjacent to the village well and pump.

As a settlement expanded the pinfold which was once on the outskirts became part of the built environment and is now often to be found on a small piece of much reduced common land surrounded by modern housing. As well as an adjacent well or pump the village stocks and the smithy could often be found nearby.

Pinfolds as an Artwork.

New interest in pinfolds and sheepfolds was aroused in Cumbria when in 1996 the artist Andy Goldsworthy, as part of the UK's Year of Visual Arts, undertook with Cumbria County Council the Sheepfold Project to renovate existing sheepfolds or re- create sheepfolds and pinfolds as art works. He used Ordnance Survey maps and local knowledge to identify sites and worked with a wide range of local organisations and individuals across Cumbria.[4] Part of the project included rebuilding pinfolds on or as near their original sites as possible and including a stone cone in the centre of them to "invigorate them with new energy". I have included these pinfolds in my listings.

How Did Pinfolds Function?

As pounds and pinfolds were established to confine stray animals found wandering on private land or on the common or waste without permission a legal framework existed to manage this function and apply sanctions

---

4   www.sheepfoldscumbria.co.uk

for misuse. This law was managed by the manor courts where the role of pinder, or pound looker, was created and an officer appointed to these jobs by the lord. Their duty was to collect straying animals and confine them in the pinfold. They guarded, fed and watered them until the owner, on payment of a fine, reclaimed them. The Manor court also imposed fines for "pound rescue" when an owner accosted the pinder and retrieved his stock, sometimes by force, as they were being led to the pinfold and "pound-breach" where the pinfold was broken into to remove impounded stock.

Straying livestock could also be driven to the pound as a public duty by anyone who found stock grazing on their fields or straggling in the lanes and byways. However the animals could only be driven to the village or manorial pinfold not to a private enclosure. This is demonstrated when in Aspatria at the court held on the 22nd day of October in the ninth year of the reign of King Henry VIII (1518) the court was presented with various offences carried out by a vicar. This particular vicar had it seems committed several offences addressed by the court. The transcription of the court hearing regarding the impounding reads:

"Also the same vicar has unlawfully imparked the cattle of the neighbours in the precincts of his vicarage to wit in the Court and not at the common enclosure (pound) as he ought to do as to nuisance and contrary to the orders".

He was also accused of:

enlarging his close by setting forward the fence on to the Lord's soil at the north end to the extent of half a rood of the Lord's land

that his servant removed divers metes and bounds between the Lord's land and the land of the Bishop of Carlisle which were set in ancient times between the dwelling house of John Murray and Stanesteill to the nuisance of the Lord's tenants.

that he has blocked up the usual way of William Harrison which was formerly assigned by the Inquisition and has fastened the gate of the same with an iron bar and with bolts and has at the said gate made diverse pits so deep that no one can go either in or out by it with any carriage.[5]

Other contemporary court records show it was a regular occurrence for people who relied on the land for a subsistence living to try to enlarge their land holding or graze their stock on other peoples land and on occasions were fined for the privilege. Also as part of the manor court business the construction, repair and other questions of law relating to the pound or pinfold were dealt with until this responsibility passed to the vestry meetings and then to parish councils.

Why did Pinfold Use Decline?

References to the impounding of animals can be found in the archives as far back as the fourteenth century and the manorial system of government encouraged and promulgated the principle of townships and smallholdings. Each peasant farmer had a few animals, typically a horse, a house cow, a few pigs and fowl and perhaps cultivated a field strip for crops from which they paid their tithe to the Lord. Good land, especially on the fell areas of Cumbria, was limited and as population increased the available land became more valuable for cropping and grazing.

During the Middle Ages the open field system of farming, with its lack of hedges and fences, saw the need to impound stray stock to safeguard grass, crops and grazing rights, especially in years of drought and disease. The manor courts appointed officials called lookers to oversee all aspects of the township such as constables, moor lookers, mill lookers, dunghill lookers, hedge lookers and pinfold lookers whose responsibility it was to ensure these features remained in good repair.

As the dry stone walls in Cumbria were built to mark the division between fields and pasture and the Enclosure Acts of the mid-eighteenth century were put in force more land was enclosed and fenced creating a countryside in less need of the function of the pinfold. As their use declined they also became neglected and were often pulled down for their stone or to create space for road widening and house building.

---

5 WRO D/LEC 299

Present Day Condition.

The visible evidence of pounds and pinfolds remaining today varies considerably. Some structures have been renovated or preserved and may boast a plaque whilst others just exist in the landscape in various states of repair. Some are listed and cared for by individuals or public bodies. Many are kept as reminders of our rural history, as monuments or as public amenity areas. Still others incorporate art works or provide enclosed gardens and some are even used to confine animals! But by far the majority only remain as marks on a map having long ago been demolished as being obsolete. The stone is often re-used elsewhere in the village for new walls and buildings.

In Field Broughton the remaining limestone coping on the pound was found to be remarkably similar to that on a nearby boundary wall built in the late eighteenth century. Many pinfolds have been restored or stabilised and the Field Broughton pound is a positive example of this. Deterioration was halted in 1980 and with Heritage Lottery Funding was restored in 2000. See before and after images below.

Before

After

Part II

Contemporary Life in the Pinfold Era

Living in Cumbria.

Cumbria, as defined in this study, is perhaps unique in that as a subdivision of England it consists of a central mountainous area almost surrounded by a lowland landscape. The central area with its upland fells and moors provided grazing but the land, especially in the fifteenth century was too poor to efficiently grow agricultural crops, in contrast to the lowlands which provided good agricultural land especially in the river valleys and around the coast

Pounds and pinfolds were situated mainly in the townships and pastoral communities of Cumbria. The small farming communities occupied the meadows and cultivated land on the coast and within the valleys and valley heads and were bordered by the unenclosed waste, moorland and upland fell areas of the County.

During the early period of pinfold use, villages, farmsteads and the ordinary peasant living in Cumbria had to contend with *war and pestilence* on a large scale. Hostilities with Scotland affected areas as far south as Penrith and the Black Death affected the more urban areas of Carlisle and especially the townships within the River Eden valley. Cattle and sheep diseases could be devastating and combined with crop failure due to climatic conditions made life for the mainly pastoral people of Cumbria very difficult.

Life from the late sixteenth century onwards saw a gradual improvement in the fortunes of the villagers, farmers, tenants and villeins and it is from the sixteenth century that a small amount of documentary evidence can be found preserved by the County's Archive Service. Although manorial law dominated for a considerable time the lord of the manor's influence gradually diminished and governance was passed to the vestry meetings. Private ownership of land became possible and many families changed from keeping animals for their own subsistence to breeding and stock farming for the market. There was a separation of woodland from grazing, permanent walls and hedges were introduced and grass and crop fields were gradually enclosed.

Land Enclosure.

It is not surprising that even by the eighteenth century most of the land in Cumbria, especially the counties of Westmorland and Cumberland, consisted of unenclosed upland waste. Where land had been improved, usually in the valley bottoms, it was enclosed with ditches, hedging or walling but this left much common and upland land in poor condition. Manorial records show that the private and illegal enclosure of small pieces of land to enlarge an existing holding often occurred both to common land and that belonging to the lord. It was a common offence brought before the court. On a larger scale tenants with a legal right to graze stock on the commons often found them in such a poor condition they petitioned the Lord requesting their division and enclosure so that they could be improved.

A petition dated 1813 was put to the *Honourable George O'Brien, Earl of Egremont, Lord of the Manor Of Braithwaite and Coledale that the Commons and Waste Grounds in their present condition are of little value but if they were divided and inclosed and specific shares thereof assigned and allotted to each Person entitled thereto and interested therof it would be greatly to the advantage of your Petitioners and all those entitled to rights of Common.* It was requested by the 25 petitioners that a bill for division and enclosure be raised and put to Parliament.[6]

The raising and presentation to Parliament of such a private bill was a complicated and expensive procedure which the General Enclosure Act of 1801 sought to simplify. Parliamentary Enclosure Awards were made in Cumbria from as early as the 1750's and continued through to the 1890's when some felt that better management of the commons was perhaps a better option than expensive enclosure and its consequences. The impact of enclosure on the need for pounds and pinfolds is difficult to judge. As land was enclosed by physical boundaries it seems likely that their usage should diminish but common land remained widespread in Cumbria. During the period when enclosure was being promulgated the number of fines imposed for not keeping the pinfold in good repair, pound rescues and breaches found in manor court records do not seem to have diminished.

---

6   WRO D/LEC 265/18

Upland and Lowland Land Use.

The requirement to grow crops for both human and animal consumption and to provide grazing for cows, sheep and pigs as well as a number of horses put extreme pressure on any suitable land in these upland counties of Cumberland, Westmorland and Lancashire. Practices developed and evolved to make best use of the fertile land in the lowland areas and exploit the availability of grass and rough grazing on the moorland and wastes. The use of sheilings and agistment became critical, where in the summer months herdsmen spent time with their animals grazing them on available grass in the hills having paid for the right to use the upland commons and wastes.

The management of the commons and wastes and the rights of tenants to graze their animals on them was critical and often contentious. Tenants of the manor were given a right of pasturage, for others payment was necessary because the use of common land for grazing was only a right if they owned land in the manor. Grazing rights were given in the form of stints. The number of stints each person was given or was able to buy varied between commons and between manors. On Newton Arlosh Common in the north of Cumbria, according to an early Commons Register 1 Stint allows for 1 beast with full mouth or 2 beasts with calf teeth or 3 beasts with 2 teeth each. 2 Stints allows for 1 horse or 5 sheep and followers, 6 geld sheep and 1 head of cattle.To cope with the variety of animals grazing it was also stipulated that 2 geese were equivalent to 1 cow and 2 cows were equivalent to 1 horse.

Having to seek permission to keep stock on the common controlled the amount of grazing and was an early conservation measure. Various agreements were put in place and policed by the manor courts who arranged for the driving of commons and wastes. Any animals found grazing unlawfully were impounded in the manorial pound until the owner had either established his right to graze or paid a fine. Even those who were entitled to graze the commons were closely watched to avoid overgrazing. The rule of levancy and couchancy was used to determine the number of animals allowed to graze by calculating the number of animals that could be kept over winter on the farm. Strict fines were imposed by the manor courts for overgrazing. In the rural townships of Cumbria under the influence of the manor courts there developed a management system whereby the court appointed officers for the overseeing of the community.

As a result nearly every township would have a pound or pinfold and some more than one.

Manors and their Role.

The Manor originated as an early unit of land management and local government. It was based on the understanding that both the Lord and his tenants had mutual rights and responsibilities which as they grew became the jurisdiction of the manorial court. The court rolls were until the mid-1600s, written in Latin and in Cumbria as in many parts of England their survival is patchy. Over the centuries the manor changed from being simply the residence of the landowner to that of a lord who held a court, a court baron and sometimes a court leet as well. It does not follow that all manors covered large tracts of land as some would only consist of one township or village.

In the earlier centuries baronial courts on behalf of the lord had jurisdiction over many aspects of life and even today principles are enshrined in statute within our modern legal system. As far back as 1267 The Statute of Marlborough lays down that no man shall take satisfaction on his own account, but only through the King's Court: that is he may seize or impound property but then be subject to legal judgement. This principle of distraint is still enshrined in the law of Great Britain and with the demise of the medieval public pound and pinfold there is now the right to impound stray cattle in the impounders stable or field until collected by the owner.

The function of the pinfold was supported by the manorial system. The manor courts were formed of jurors appointed by the court. These were made up of landowners and were responsible for the appointment of the pinder and other "keepers" and "lookers". They were also responsible for imposing fines or ammerces.

In the Manor of Cockermouth a handwritten account of court proceedings dated 1698[7] records that the main business of the court that day was to appoint the officials of the court. The names of the appointed jurors, nineteen in number, is followed by the appointment of the bailiffe and constables as well as the hedge lookers, moor lookers, mill lookers, pinfold lookers, swine ringers and many others.

---

7   WRO D/LEC 103

The chief role was that of bailiffe. In the court leet rolls of the Honour and Manor of Cockermouth dated Saturday the 30th day of September 1775 "Before Thomas Benson Gentleman Deputy Steward" for "the Right Honourable George, Earl of Egremont and Baron of Cockermouth" Mr John Lucock was presented to be bailiff of the borough of Cockermouth for the next year. An oath was administered and signed by John Lucock which read:

"You shall so far as you will well and truly serve our Sovereign Lord the King and The Lord of This Borough in the office of Bailiff of the said Borough of Cockermouth for the year ensuing and well and truly Collect all such rents and other annual Profits as shall be chargeable and owing out of the said Borough and there of make and give an absolute Account at the end of same year And also shall duly Execute all such proceedings as shall come out of the Lord's Court there to you directed; and in Every other thing belonging to your office well and truly discharge your office this year coming,[8]

So help you God

The other key role was that of constable whose duties varied between manors but this 1801 extract from the accounts of the constable for Threlkeld, John Thompson, shows these included some pinfold duties

A Bill of Money laid out in doing the office of constable in the Hamlet of Threlkeld for one year by John Thompson 1801 reads:

---

8   WRO D/LEC 116

To the Rev.d Mr Law for giving the oath to a list of the Freeholders resident within the Constablewick of Threlkeld	1s 0d
John Cochbane bill for making a new gate to the pinfold and nails	2s 6d
Robert Hollyday bill for his work	1s 9d
To repairing the wall	1s 6d
To Relieving poor Distressed Travellers By order of the Magistrate	11s 4d
	18s 1d[9]

Other appointments in the Manor of Threlkeld for the year were, *assessors, hedge lookers, assessors of bread and wine, mill lookers, market lookers, moor lookers, leather searchers, appraisors, swine ringers, dunghill lookers and pinfold lookers.*

The term "looker" was used by the manor courts to denote an official appointment to oversee a particular aspect of manor law and present offenders to the court. A ' hedge looker' ensured that hedged field boundaries were kept in good repair and a pinfold looker would regularly inspect the pinfold to ensure it was fit for purpose.

The pinder was a separate appointment and one of many appointments made by the manor courts. Local landowners and representatives of the lord made up the jurors of the court who heard and decided on the business put before them. Although there are many entries describing the poor condition of the pinfolds some manor courts adopted the practice of recording that the pinfold or pound was in good condition. Recorded no doubt to support the work of the looker and the pinder.

9 CRO PC 21/2

Part III

The Management of Pounds and Pinfolds.

Evidence of Management.

I have already noted the interchangeable use of the term pound and pinfold and the similarity of sheepfolds to pounds and pinfolds and therefore the tendency to confuse them. The written evidence can also be misleading as the vernacular language soon becomes part of everyday language rather than referenced to the historical evidence. However my research has clearly shown there are certain indicators within the features of a pound and pinfold that can be applied to differentiate them from a sheepfold or any other type of walled enclosure. These are structural appearance, location and availability of a water source. There are several examples of a pinfold being marked on a map where I believe it should be more properly referred to as a sheepfold or other structure. In view of this and as the terms pound and pinfold and their derivatives have a long history of usage I have accepted that there is not a clear rule and perhaps it should be taken that the contemporary name applied to such a structure is the appropriate term. This is the approach I have adopted and used in this research.

Early primary source material for the management of pounds and pinfolds in Cumbria is minimal but does exist in the archives. I have used the manor court records held in the Leconfield archive at Cockermouth Castle and other references found by examination of the various on-line and archive indexes and catalogues. The early manorial records were written in Latin during the sixteenth century until an early type of English was used throughout the seventeenth and eighteenth centuries.

As the pinfold fell into disuse from about the mid-nineteenth century their management lapsed and many became derelict. Some were sold and demolished, some stayed in the ownership of the lord of the manor and their successors and still others passed through vestry ownership to the parish councils. Written records from parish councils varies in detail, as does their interest in the pinfold, and a common trend found was their repeated attempts to keep them free from fly tipping and in good condition. The nineteenth century saw some improvement as public and council interest in heritage increased and funds were made available for the restoration of pounds and pinfolds. I have noted aspects of this process against specific entries in the register of Cumbrian pounds and pinfolds.

The Need for a Pound or Pinfold.

An early reference to the need for control of stray stock to protect grazing quality and the solution found is in the records of the *"Court of Brackenthwaite held on the Thursday next after the Feast of St Kyntigirnin (13ᵗʰ January) in the 13ᵗʰ year of the reign of King Edward IV."* (1413)

It is recorded that it was found by the Inquisition of John Mires, John Rudd, William Hodgson (and others) that *"Lorton Heders to be inclosed and kept inclosed during the open season and there the neighbours stray cattle may be driven".*

This order applied to an area of land in Lorton put aside specifically for the open season when the commons could be grazed. A pound or pinfold was both a practical and an economic necessity in any township or hamlet where livestock were kept and inevitably strayed, sometimes deliberately I suspect, from their owners land to the lush grass of a neighbour's. Pasture was often unenclosed and those fences and walls that did exist could easily be breached. Pinfolds were also used as a means of destraint for rent when the animals owned were often a family's chief and only asset. Although cattle and sheep were the main types of animal impounded in the counties within this study there was also a need to impound pigs, horses and no doubt geese and fowl. These conditions applied to much of the populated valleys and fell side areas of Cumbria and so pounds and pinfolds were found in nearly every township and manor.

The confining of stray animals was but a small part of the manor court business. The same entry in the Court of Brackenthwaite rolls demonstrates this and gives an insight to other court business. It is recorded that:

Peter Skynner be fined 4d for keeping 20 foreign sheep;

the family of the wife of William Wilkynson fined 8d for keeping 20 sheep,

that Thomas Robynson be fined 2s for shedding the blood of John Newcom and

John Tollyson fined for removing the course of the water called Rede Moss Beck.

These offences give a flavour of life as it was lived at the time and shows that the manor court was the body that upheld the law when pounds and pinfolds were a necessary part of rural subsistence living in Cumbria.

Construction of a Pound or Pinfold.

The responsibility for the building or rebuilding of a pound rested with the lord of the manor, his tenants or the township and in some cases it was a joint responsibility. The structure needed to be capable of securely holding a number of animals and of withstanding damage from the stock confined in it and on occasion from the stock owners trying to rescue their animals to avoid the fine. Manorial evidence shows that tenants often made petition to the manorial lord for the establishment and erection of a pinfold or its repair when they thought it was necessary and beneficial to themselves and to his manor.

This is an example of a manor court record dated 1748 which in its preamble introduces the business of the court states when and where it was held and who the jurors were. In amongst other business I found the order made to fund the repair of the pinfold at Dean.[10]

The record reads: The Manor of Dean and Whinfell

The Court Baron and customary Court of the most Noble Lord Charles Duke of Somerset, Marquise & Earl of Hertford, Viscount and Baron Beauchamp, Lord of the Honours of Cockermouth and Chancellor of the University of Cambridge, Lord High Steward of the city of Chichester, One of the Governors of the Chamber House, Knight of the most Noble Order of the Garter and one of the Lords of his Majesty's most Honourable Privy Council:

Holder of (Held in) the School House in Dean for the said Manors on Thursday the Fourteenth Day of April 1748 before Thomas Simpson Gentleman Steward of the said Courts,

The names of the Jurors by the aforesaid have all sworn to enquire for the Lord of the said Manor and to present all and singular the Matter and Things which to the said Courts do belong and appertain...

---

10 WRO D/LEC 116

Henry Lancaster	*Wm Wood*	*Thomas Wood*
Jeremiah Head	*John Bayle*	*John Shearman*
Christopher Baile	*John Pearson*	*John Wilson*
Jonathan Wilson	*Richard Lancaster*	*Henry Walker*
Jon Stainton		*Richard Head*

All sworn

Which said Jurors upon their Oaths say and profound as follows…

The pinfold belonging to the Town of Dean being much out of repair We the Jury, whose names are underwritten do order that every Person having land or parcel within or belonging to the Town of Dean, or to Croft Houses, Woodhall, Parsonage and Woodside do contribute towards raising a Sum for repairing thereof according to each survey rate.

There are several examples of petitions being drawn up and presented to the lord of the manor by his tenants. This petition, dated 1816, from the tenants of the Manor of Calbeck, Upton and Underfell requested that Lord Egremont pay his proportion of the expenses of repairing the pinfold.[11] It reads:

To the right honourable George O'Brian Earl of Egremont and Baron of Cockermouth.

The Petition of the Tenants of your Lordships Manors of Caldbeck Upton and Underfell in the County of Cumberland.

Sheweth, That there is within the said Manors a large Tract of unenclosed Common upon which your Petitioners have a right of Pasturage. That in order to preserve their Rights, your Petitioners together with your Lordship's Bailiff have at different times driven the said Common and impounded the Cattle of such Persons as had no Right of Pasturage upon the said Commons.

---

11   WRO D/LEC 265/11

That your Petitioners believe that your Lordship's Predecessors, Lords of said Manors when the pound or pinfold was built or repaired, have been accustomed to erect the Door and Door-Case, and so much of the Wall, as with the Door and Door-Case came to one half of the whole Expense.

Your Petitioners therefore pray that your Lordship will direct your Agents in the County of Cumberland to pay one half or such other Proportion of the Expense of the annexed estimate for rebuilding the pound, as to your Lordship shall seem meet.

Estimate of the Expense of building a pound. The pound to be circular, of 13 Yards Diameter, the Wall to be 7½ Feet high, And the Content of the Wall 100 Square Yards:

100 Yards at 3/9 per Yard £18:15s:0d,
Door Case £1:10s:0d,
Door & Lock £1: 5s:0d,
Amount of Expense £21:10S:0d

Signed on behalf of your Lordship's Tenants within the said Manors the 6ᵗʰ December 1816 by 16 tenants.

It seems that this particular pound needed rebuilding and put in use to safeguard the tenants' rights to pasturage on the common and facilitate the impounding of cattle belonging to those who have no such right of pasturage. pounds were clearly used to control grazing rights on the commons and wastes and in this particular petition the dimensions and costs of rebuilding are given. Optimistically perhaps the lord is asked for one half of the cost or *"such other proportion"* that the lord deemed fit to pay.

I have found two records of pinfolds in this manor, A small one at Potts Gills (see image) and another at Town Head which may be the subject of this petition. Caldbeck Town Head pound was situated to the south-east of the village. It is at the junction of several tracks coming in from the improved agricultural land adjacent to the fells. It was close to a spring and its proximity to the fell would facilitate

the impounding of animals found grazing on open fell without permission.

In the Barony of Brugh (Burgh-by-Sands) a similar petition is signed by at least thirty six inhabitants of the Barony but for a different reason to that given by the Caldbeck petition. In this slightly later petition the inhabitants are concerned about the damage done by the trespass of animals deliberately turned out on to the roads and lanes and then allowed to graze on the fields.

It reads:

Barony of Brugh June 23rd 1819.

We the Undersigned being Inhabitants of the Barony of Brugh having taken into consideration the Damage done by Individuals within the said Barony by People who turn their Cattle, Horses etc into the High Roads and lanes within the said Barony whereby several trespasses have been committed upon the fields of the Inhabitants adjoining the said Highways and lanes we therefore think it necessary to have a pinfold erected within the Barony to prevent such trespass in future.[12]

The response to this petition is not known as no pinfold in the ancient Barony of Brugh could be traced. The Barony of Brugh was created in 1092, has been held by eight northern families over the last 900 years. It was passed by female descent through the D'Estrivers, Engaines, Morvilles, Lucies, de Multons, Dacres and Howards before being sold in 1685 by the Duke of Norfolk to Sir John Lowther, whose descendants the Earls of Lonsdale have held the title ever since.

Appointment of Pinders and Lookers.

The pinder, also referred to as pounder or pinner, was appointed by the manor court which supported him in disputes and on the occasions when he suffered physical injury. The pinder's role was to round up straying animals and drive them to the pound. He may in some manors also have the responsibility to maintain the pound. While stock were impounded he fed, watered and protected them until the owner paid a fine, imposed by the manor court, which was deemed sufficient to cover the costs of their keep and the pinder's wages.

The pinder was one of many appointments made by the manor courts and these were on one occasion appointed en masse in Caldbeck where

---

12 WRO D LONS L5/2/41/155

Thomas Scott, Daniel Hodge, Jonathan Sheperd, Joshua Harrison and a second Thomas Scott were all appointed pounders for various pounds within the Calbeck manor. Local landowners and representatives of the lord made up the jurors of the court who heard and decided on the business put before them.

In the Manor of Cockermouth the handwritten account of court proceedings dated 1696 records the names of the jurors who formed the "Inquisition". They appointed lookers, including pinfold lookers, who were the men with special responsibility to oversee the condition and use of the pound or pinfold on behalf of the court. The lookers were often unpopular as they were also responsible for bringing offenders before the court.

A unique example of a vestry meeting seeking to appoint a pinder is found in a document dated 25th August 1842. In it the Poor Law Commissioners at Somerset House, London, seek the approval of the Brampton Poor House Union to appoint George Harrison, an inmate in the Brampton Workhouse, as pinder for Brampton. The Commissioners quote an entry in the vestry book as follows:

"At an adjourned Vestry meeting of the parish of Brampton held this 15th day of July 1842 for the purpose of appointing a person to take into and impound all Cattle, Horses, Pigs etc at large on the streets and highways in the said Parish. It was resolved that application be made to the Board of Guardians of the Brampton Union requesting them to allow George Harrison to take into and impound all horses be going at large in the highways in this parish and also prevent Hawkers, Higglers, Gipsies or other persons to encamp upon any part of the said Highways and that George Harrison be allowed all fines for the same".

The Commissioners response stated that George Harrison had been an inmate at the Brampton Workhouse for the last 6 years, is about 50 years of age but infirm and unable to do any labour save walking about. Despite this they confirmed his appointment as pinder.

The act of identifying stray stock and driving them to the pound was not the sole reserve of the appointed pinder as any person could identify stray stock and place them in the pound. This led to several interesting situations coming before the manor mourts.

In an early account of the Aspatrike (Aspatria) Court held on 22nd October 1518 the jurors were very busy considering many offences concerning the use of the waste and commons. Fines were imposed for removing numerous wagon loads of turf for fuel, for keeping pigs on the common and moving fences. In particular a vicar, whose name cannot be deciphered, was shown as having:

> "Enlarged his close called the Flatt and has set forward the fence on to the Lords soil at the north end of the same close to the extent of half a wood adding it to the land of the Bishop of Carlisle. Also the said vicar has by his servant removed divers metes and bounds between the Lords land and the land of the Bishop of Carlisle which were set in ancient times to the nuisance of the Lords tenants and blocked up the usual way of William Harrison and has fastened a gate with an iron bar and bolts".[13]

He also set up his own version of the common pound:

> "Also the same vicar has unlawfully imparked the cattle of the neighbours in the precincts of his vicarage to wit in the Courtt (courtyard) and not at the common pound as he ought to do so, to the common nuisance and contrary to orders".

Another dispute was recorded on 19th May 1518 at the Five Towns Court where:

> "John Jakson of Clifton complains of William Hyne of Graysone in a plea of trespass to wit for that the same def't did unlawfully impark a cow of the said plaintiff of the value of 12s in the Inclosure of Graysothen whereby the same plaintiff did lose his cow aforesaid from which his damage is 40d, def't denies wherefore an Inquisition plaintiff recovers nothing because def't is not to blame therefore plaintiff in mercy".

In this case the cow was deemed to have been properly impounded so the plaintiff received no recompense. The record shows he was also fined 2d.

Poundloose and Fines.

When the pinder or pounder was appointed to his position by the manor court he was reliant on the Lord of the Manor for his income. This came from the amersements, fines imposed by the court and from the poundloose, payment made to him by the Lord's tenants for release of

---

13   WRO D/LEC 299/24

their livestock. This income would also provide for the cost of feeding the impounded stock until their release. Payment to the pinder is confirmed in the agreement to appoint the pinder at Brampton, described above, where he is to receive the income from the fines imposed by the court.

However it seems that the pounder was bypassed by two enterprising free tenants of the Lord of Dundraw who took it on themselves to impound cattle and collect the poundloose for their own profit:

> *The Wigton Court held on the 23rd day of May in the 23rd year of the reign of King Henry VIII (1533)... Although the lord is entitled to fines from foreign cattle notwithstanding this certain tenants to wit Thomas Lamplughtt of Dovenby and Richard Briscow of Croften and William Mertindale chaplain of the free tenants of the lord of Dundraw and Whirig and by the titles of the same attach foreign cattle and take the poundloose for the same otherwise than they ought and are accustomed. Fine 40s.[14]*

The fine of 40s is a significant amount and expresses strongly the Wigton Courts displeasure at the attempted usurping of their power and the misdirection of funds that should be theirs.

Pound Rescue and Pound Breach.

The activity of the pinder when driving stray cattle, horses or pigs to the pound was not without risk. These livestock were a valuable resource for the peasant farmer who could ill afford to be fined for letting his stock stray or even pay the cost of their keep in the pound. There are numerous and regular entries in the manorial records examined that show a fine for "rescue" or "pound-breach". These terms are often interchanged when recorded in court rolls but generally Rescue occurs when the stock is retrieved, sometimes by force, from the pinder as he is driving it to the pound and before it is impounded. Livestock is not legally impounded until it is secured in the pound so this sometimes aggressive action would it was hoped save a fine. pound-breach or as it sometimes described Foldbreak or foldbreach is where stock has been retrieved from the pound by breaking in and removing it. Many pound walls were over 6 feet in height to keep the animals in but this height was also necessary to try to discourage attempts, evidently not very successfully, at pound-breach.

---

14   WRO D/LEC 299/19/20

At the manor court the offence of rescue and that of pound-breach was often shown to be an act carried out against the court official, the bailiff, with the offender being named and fined.

An early example reads:

"Derwent Fell Court held on the 7th day of November in the third year of the reign of King Henry the Seventh (1488) the Bailiff presents John Bank Keld for 1 rescue made on the bailiff Thomas Blaykthuayt near the gate for the keeping of 2 stots (pigs). Fine 10d"

The Derwent Fells Manor covered the townships Brackenthwite, Buttermere, Embleton, Lorton, Loweswater, Mosser, Pardshaw, Whinfell and Wythop. This extract indicates that the pigs were rescued at the gate to the pound and so saved the pinders costs but incurred the court fine.

On occasions it seems that servants were sent to retrieve impounded stock for their master but on this occasion, as was the custom, it was the master who was fined 12d.

"Capital Court of Derwentfell held on the eight day of October in the 12th year of the reign of King Edward IV (1473)... Brackenthwayt presents John Strib for his servant for 1 foldbreach against John Tomlynson junior". [15]

Dean Court was part of the Five Towns Manor that included Brigham, Eaglesfield, Greysouthern and Clifton. At Dean Manor Court held on 2nd September in the 20th year of the reign of King Henry VIII (1529) amongst the many fines imposed there is an entry which reads:

"Also they present the wife of William Walker for a foldbreach 40d contrary to the penalties and Roger Rawlynge for 1 foldbreak, 40d". [16]

The wife of William Walker is not named but the fine was quite considerable. Perhaps this is another example where an attempt to stop these offences from becoming a regular occurrence is attempted by imposing punitive fines.

An entry in the Papcastle Court records a few years later on tenth day of October in the twenty third year of the reign of King Henry VIII (1533)

---

15   WRO D/LEC 299/8/10

16   WRO D/LEC 299/19/20

shows a similar fine and a list of the animals that had been found grazing or straying illegally. They were found on cow pasture out of season causing damage to the grass and thus offending rural farming law and practice at the time.

"Also they present Thomas Lamplughtt of Doven by his servant for 1 foldbreach (40d), and for 12 pigs, 16 sheep and 30 geese on cow pasture of the neighbourhood at the several season" Fine 2s.[17]

Orders to Repair of the Pound or Pinfold.

Once built the responsibility for the maintenance and repair of the pinfold was often problematical and could be subject to an order by the manor court. These orders were either to repair the pinfold by a stipulated date or to pay a fine for not having kept it in good condition. The references to the pinfold being in need of repair and the demands for its repair largely although not exclusively come from the authorities.

In the manor of Muchland in Furness the pinfold was the responsibility of the township and the court leet on 22nd October 1625, ordered the repair of the Gleaston pinfold in the following terms:

"We order that the pinfould at gleaston shall be made able by all the towne before the 6 daie of maie next upon paine of 6s 8d".[18]

This order of the court leet puts the responsibility firmly with the township to repair the pinfold and gives a date by which it should be done albeit in 6 months time. The site of the Gleaston pinfold cannot be confirmed but the 1889 OS 1,2500 map shows a site named as a sheepfold.

In the manor of Cockermouth the account of court proceedings dated 1696 records the order:

"Amercy Francis Plaskett and Henry Ramfrey for neglect of keeping the Pinfould in sufficient repair 3s 4d.[19]

As these two names are not those shown as newly appointed pinfold lookers it is not known if these were two previously appointed pinders or

---

17   WRO D/LEC 299/19/20

18   BRO BD/HJ/202/8

19   WRO D/LEC 103

two representative villagers. However manor court records examined for 1697 and 1698 record pinfold lookers names as Cho. Plasket and John Plaskett respectively, so perhaps they were pinders responsible for the pinfold as many such occupations were handed down through families.

The pound at Buttermere was cited at the court leet on 16th October 1719 as being in need of repair. Here a fine was imposed on the inhabitants:

"Turnmen of Buttermer present the pound fold gate lyeing down and Amercie the inhabitatnts of the township 6s 8d"[20]

In the manor of Dean and Whinfell the court baron made an order on 14th April 1748 which specifically set out conditions to repair and maintain their pinfold:-

The pinfold belonging to the Town of Dean being much out of repair We the Jury, whose names are underwritten do order that every Person having land or parcel within or belonging to the Town of Dean, or to Croft Houses, Woodhall, Parsonage(Pardshaw) and Woodside do contribute towards raising a Sum for repairing thereof according to each of such persons survey rate to be collected and in case any person makes use of the said pinfold, not being a contributor as above such person for every time they shall make use thereof shall pay the sum of four pence to the pounder to be applied towards the future Repairs thereof, And in case any person who ought to be a contributor as above shall neglect or refuse to pay his proportion towards such repairs do amerse such person in the sum of thirteen shillings and four pence for such neglect.[21]

This is an unusual arrangement where residents and landowners are ordered to contribute to its repair and non-resident users of the pinfold are expected to contribute to future repairs or face a fine. Unfortunately the site of Dean pinfold could not be found.

At Bolton it was the Bailiff of Bolton, Jacob Stamper, who was responsible for the repair of the Bolton pinfold and submitted his account to Cockermouth Castle, the seat of Lord Egremont. He acknowledged receipt on 18th December 1782 for the following expenses:[22]

---

20   WRO D/LEC 35A

21   WRO D/LEC 116

22   WRO D/LEC 89

29 July 1781 Paid John Hewitson for a door   0 - 5s – 0d

17 Dec 1781 Paid George Graham for Iron Work   <u>0 – 2s – 7d</u>

<u>£ 0 – 7s – 7d</u>

A similar arrangement is shown in the 1801 accounts for Threlkeld where the constable John Thompson of the hamlet of Threlkeld drew 2s 6d from the court to pay John Cockbane's bill for making a new gate and nails for the pinfold.[23]

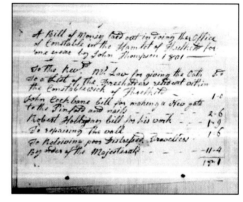

As late as 1902 there is correspondence about the pinfold between the representatives of the lord of the manor for Egremont and the solicitors responsible for the estate. Although it is unlikely that the pinfold was still in use there is obviously a responsibility of care which resulted in the order given to repair the pinfold. The work needed was described as:

> *"A portion of the wall on the south side of the pinfold has fallen. A new door is also required as the old one is completely done. The cost of repairing the wall would be 28/-s and a new door with lock say 12/-s"*[24]

The go ahead to repair the pinfold was given within three days. In the letter it mentions that the repair raises both manorial and mineral questions and that "little acts of ownership are often found useful". This is perhaps a hint that the site is of value and that although ownership is not clear it might be in Lord Egremont's future interest to maintain the structure.

The amount of the fine imposed by the manor court varied and as pointed out some fines may have been deliberately punitive but throughout the manor court records examined the amounts of 6s 8d and 13s 4d occur very frequently. This use of these specific amounts probably dates back to the noble, a coin first issued in 1344 and valued at 6 shillings and 8 pence

---

23   CRO PC/21/2

24   WRO D/LEC 280/35

or a third of a pound. A half noble was worth 3 shillings and 4 pence or a sixth of a pound. The amount also referred to the mark which although never a coin was used as a unit of account worth 13 shillings and 4 pence, two thirds of a pound.

Demise of the Pound or Pinfold.

The need to impound livestock lessened but did not disappear over time as hedges and walls were built and common land enclosed. The laws of restraint were modernised and the responsibility for the management of pinfolds, originally with the lord of the manor and the manorial courts, passed to the church vestry meetings and then to parish and town councils. The whole legal framework slowly became obsolete and along with the physical pinfold structure gradually fell into disuse. The pinfolds building material often being "recycled" legally and illegally to other building projects.

These changes were gradual and took place over many years. Ownership issues around the pinfold and the land on which it stood frequently arose and were complicated by the lack of clarity over the legal responsibilities of ownership.

The Ecclesiastical Commissioner Act of 1826 and subsequent statutes amongst other questions sought to clarify the laws on tenancy and end the practice of lifehold tenure of church property which many enjoyed. It appears that a number of pinfolds that still existed had fallen into disrepair and in 1880 the Commissioners sought Counsel Opinion on their obligations and duties in respect of them.[25]

The submission states that *"pounds have become practically obsolete and that it would be desirable to get rid of them especially in cases where the site is valuable as being surrounded by enclosed lands."* The questions raised by the Commissioners and Counsels opinion was as follows:

1st Question: Whether the Commissioners are at liberty to pull down existing pounds. Counsel: *Where there is local custom to use a pound the owner of the soil would not be able to pull down the pound.*

2nd Question: Whether they can pull down existing pounds if they substitute for them other pounds. *Counsel: If customary rights exist then no substitution would avail.*

---

25   WRO D/LEC 293/35

3rd Question: Whether they are at liberty to appropriate other waste lands in the Manors as Sites for substituted pounds. *Counsel: Lords are entitled to appropriate portions of their land for pounds provided there is a necessity for a new pound.*

4th Question: If pounds are fallen into decay whether the Commissioners can be compelled to reinstate them and if so whether by any other process than Mandamus. *Counsel: The Lord might rebuild it as a matter of ordinary favour to his tenants.*

5th Question: Whether the Commissioners can sell as absolute freehold the sites of pounds surrounded by enclosed lands which have become partly or wholly disused or for which other sites have been substituted. *Counsel: The Limitations Act would apply. Whether the pound was partly or wholly disused would affect a custom to use. If no custom exists then the pound is treated as freehold property of the Manor.*

6th Question: Whether any distinction exists between the pounds in lifehold Manors and those in Manors of inheritance as regards any of the above mentioned questions. *Counsel: There is no distinction.*

I have abbreviated Counsels response above but it seems that in essence local custom set an all important precedent and if this did not exist the Commissioners *"could deal with the sites of any pounds within their Manors as they please".*

As late as 1843 the law relating to pounds and pinfolds was still being considered when a bill on pound-breach and Rescue was discussed in Parliament. This was an act to amend the law relating to these issues and laid down that:

> *"any person or persons that shall release or attempt to release any horse, ass, sheep, swine, or other beast or cattle, which shall be lawfully seized for the purpose of being impounded, in consequence of having been found wandering, straying or lying or being depastured on any inclosed land without the consent of the owner or occupier of such inclosed land, from the pound or place where the same shall be so impounded, or on the way to or from any such pound or place or shall pull down, damage or destroy the same pound or place or any part thereof or any lock or bolt belonging thereto or with which the same shall be fastened every person so offending shall upon conviction before any two of Her Majesty's*

Justices of the Peace, forfeit and pay any sum not exceeding Five pounds, together with reasonable charges and expenses, or in default thereof be committed by Warrant to the house of correction there to be kept to hard labour for up to three calendar months nor less than 14 days".[26]

In some instances pinfolds were being sold:

An agents letter to Lord Leconfield, Cockermouth Castle dated 23rd March 1886 is asking if the pinfold at Great Broughton may be sold to the owner of an adjoining property. It seems here that the overseers had offered the sale without consulting Lord Leconfield the owner.

The immediate outcome of this correspondence is not known but today the pinfold is owned by the parish council who rent it as a garden to the adjoining residence.

Another example of a pinfold being sold and the issues involved with such a sale is the pinfold at Setmurthy in the manor of Derwentfells which had been out of use for many years according to a letter dated June 17 1890. This letter explains that a Canon Hoskins has purchased the shooting rights over the land on which the dilapidated pinfold stands and would now like to purchase the pinfold and land (ref 227) on which it stands from Lord

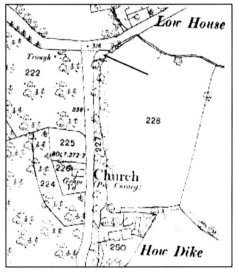

Leconfield. (See image) This was agreed and a conveyance was drawn up and signed on the 4th day of May 1891 selling the land and pinfold to Canon Hoskins for five shillings with the condition:

Excepting and reserving to the said Henry Baron Leconfield and his successors in estate that Richard Hoskins hereby grants to him all the gravel clay brick earth stone iron ore and all mines minerals mineral and other substances whatsoever lying and being within and under the

26 Parliamentary Papers Online

said piece of land together with full and absolute power for the said Henry Baron Leconfield and his successors in estate and his and their tenant to dig for get to work even manufacture and carry away without being liable to pay any Compensation whatsoever for surface subsidence or the erection of machinery proper for getting the said sand and gravel clay brick earth stone iron ore mines minerals and mineral and other substances or any of them.[27]

Today all that remains of the pinfold is part of the wall at the end of a narrow strip of steep woodland bordering a stream. I could find no evidence of mineral extraction!

In their time Cumbrian pinfolds served a very useful purpose in reducing damage to pasturage caused by stray livestock and were an essential tool in enforcing manor court rules. At the same time employment was provided for pinders and lookers and they providing an income for the manor. They also caused controversy through pound rescues and pound-breaches and of course the implementation of fines by the manor courts. Even when they were no longer required their legal status was not clear and certainly their ownership was on many occasions in doubt.

This study has shown that of the pounds and pinfolds that can still be found in Cumbria ownership varies between private, parish council and National Park. Most are kept in a recognisable state, many with information plaques and a good number being used as a private garden or community amenity. Inevitably some are in need of attention before they disappear completely, which is my next task!

---

27   CRO SL 51/4

Part IV.

The Pound and Pinfold Today

Methodology.

Sources available to me initially included the Listed Building Register, First Edition Ordnance Survey maps, Internet searches and local knowledge. The Lake District National Park Authority and the Friends of The Lake District were both helpful in allowing me to use some of their reference material to identify structures that I may not have otherwise located. Of particular help was the Cumbria Association of Local Councils (CALC) who circulated a flyer for me asking local parish councils for their help in identifying pounds and pinfolds in their parish.

Archive research was initially facilitated with the support of the Lorton & Derwent Fells Local History Society and guidance from Lancaster University. Access to the Leconfield Archive held at Cockermouth Castle was made available to me through Whitehaven Records office. It is from this source and other Cumbria County Council Archive services that most written evidence was found.

My website www.pounds and pinfolds.co.uk was valuable in prompting members of the public to tell me or ask me about pounds and pinfolds and now contains the National Register of pounds and pinfolds.

Contemporary Comment.

My research has shown that on the one hand there is a lack of knowledge about these structures and on the other hand I think a growing interest in preserving them for future generations. This interest is shown in the number that are listed by English Heritage, by the number that are maintained by the Lake District National Park and by the more numerous examples that are preserved and looked after by parish councils throughout Cumbria.

Although the nature and need for the function of the pound and pinfold examined here has long since disappeared the concept of impounding property, whether it be animals or possessions, has persisted not just in the public memory but has manifested itself in common practice. In the letters section of The Times in 1908 it was suggested that the principle of impounding should also be applied to the cars of drivers *who drive at a speed dangerous to the public.* It is said that every driver of a horse drawn carriage is subject to conviction and so also should a car driver *because they are not a privileged class.* The offending car, it is suggested, should be impounded *for a time proportionate to the gravity of the offence.*

In 1823 the Times also reported an incident where unattended horses in the streets of London had become a nuisance and the Beadles decided to do something about it. Having noticed two horses causing a nuisance they removed them to the green-yard (pound) and demanded a penalty of 21s mitigated to 11 s if paid immediately without reference to the Magistrate. The owners paid up and then vindictively took their case to the Magistrate who reprimanded the Beadles and ordered them to pay the costs of the hearing. The horse owners received no compensation as the magistrate had determined that it was proved that they had in fact rightly incurred the penalty.

Straying stock still posed a problem in 2004 when the Westmorland Gazette reported that the police had issued a stray stock warning. The report emphasises the need to keep fences and walls in good repair as straying stock can cause accidents. It points out that it is an offence under the 1980 Highways Act to allow animals to stray onto a highway and that failure to do this could result in an appearance in court, and a fine but there is no mention of what happens to the stock!

On more than one occasion when trying to locate pinfolds in the towns and villages of Cumbria I heard the view that the threat of impounding strays in pinfolds should be brought back into use to encourage good animal management and it was even suggested that it should not be limited to animals!

The Pinfold in Our Culture.

The pound, or more specifically the pinder, features in literature as far back as the seventeenth century in the poem *The Jolly Pinder of Wakefield* one of the stories that surround Robin Hood. In this poem the pinder is a town official trying to ensure that the crops are safeguarded only to find them being trampled by Robin and his men. John Clare in his pastoral poem *The Shepherd's Calendar* published in 1827 also refers to the role of the pound and pinder in the life of the countryside.

In the 1970 film *Ned Kelly* starring Mick Jagger an early event portrayed in the film shows the gang breaking out horses from the pound and adding this offence to an already long string of offences he has allegedly committed.

The most significant reminder of the pound and pinfold is perhaps the number of houses, roads, avenues, closes and even towns that now bear the name of pound or pinder. They are certainly too numerous to research or even count and are probably so named not because there is a pound or pinfold there but that it was demolished to make way for what now exists!

Part V.

The Listings

C   Abbey Town pound, Wigton.
Grid ref: 317391,5506847
It is located on the left approaching
Abbey Town from the south on the
B5302, at the far end of a row of
terraced houses. This is a stone pound
with triangular capping stones and a
small iron gate with overhead lintel.

In good order, now used as a garden and approx. 10mtrs by 7mtrs.
The south corner has been removed and wall rebuilt probably to
give rear access to the row of houses. It is shown on the 1866 OS
1:2500 map, as a pound in the corner of a field. No buildings are
shown. A date stone on the adjacent row of houses indicates they
were built in 1887 and the removal of the south corner of the
pinfold probably occurred then.

S   Ainstable pinfold, Penrith. No trace. Grid ref: 352581,546414.
Shown as a pinfold on the 1868 OS 1:10,560 map. The road has
been widened at the site and the pinfold has been lost.

NF   Ambleside. No trace. Grid ref: 337700,504600.
Possible site is where Pinfold Garage is now built. No trace found
on OS maps.

S   Anthorn Bridge pinfold, Wigton. No trace. Grid ref:
319495,558237. Shown as a pinfold on the 1868 OS 1:10,560 map
but site now occupied by a Community Hall.

C   Appleby – Bondgate pinfold. Grid ref: 369130,519980
This pinfold is named on the 1859 1:2,500 OS map on the edge of an area of strip fields. It is unusual to have the building as part of the pinfold and this may have been added as a practical facility when its original function was no longer required.

NF   Appleby – Scattergate pinfold. No trace. Grid ref: 368110,519840.Shown as a pinfold on the 1859 OS 1:2,500 map but site position not clear. Possible site now surrounded by modern housing.

S   Armathwaite pinfold, Penrith. No trace. Grid ref: 350641,546269. Shown as a pinfold on the 1868 OS 1:10,560 map but site is now clear. Existing field walls and fallen stones may be part of original pinfold.

S   Aspatria pinfold. No trace. Grid ref: 314280,541811. Shown as a large square pinfold on the 1883-87 OS 1:2,500 map on a site now occupied by Aspatria School.

S   Barbon pinfold. No trace. Grid ref: 362500,482168. The pinfold is shown on the County Series 1st Edition OS map of 1862 close to a small stream. The site is now part of a field. Landowner has no knowledge of a pinfold on the site.

C   Bassenthwaite. (Kilnhill) Grid ref: 321664,532556. Shown on the 1895 1:2,500 OS map this pinfold is hidden away in a small thicket and in poor repair.

NF   Beckside, Ireleth. No trace.
      Archive reference to Pinfold Parrock sold. No trace on OS maps.

P   Bewaldeth pinfold, Bassenthwaite. Grid ref: 321012,534866.
      Located on private land belonging to Low Garth Farm, Bewaldeth
      and shown as a pinfold on the 1867 & 1886 OS maps but as
      a Sheepfold on the 1900 OS 1:2,500 map. It is in a dilapidated
      condition and stands in what is now a wet marshy area. Unusually
      it has two gateways and may have been the manorial pound for
      the manor house at Low Garth Farm. It is ideally located for this
      function as it is near the foot of a track heading towards open fell.
      Further along the fell track are the remains of an ancient Friends
      Meeting House and burial ground.

P   Bleatarn pinfold, Warcop. Grid ref: 373194,513635
      Located to the south of the hamlet of Bleatarn this circular pinfold
      is shown on the 1898 OS 1:2,500 map sited on a small piece of
      unfenced land, possibly common land, adjacent to a small stream
      feeding the River Eden. The site has since been walled to define the
      road and part of the pinfold lost as a result.

C   Blindbothel pinfold, Lorton. (Whinfell). Grid ref: 314413,525795
      Located beside the cross fell track over Whinfell to Mosser. This
      ancient way would have provided a direct route from the Lorton
      Vale to the fertile valley fields of Mosser and access to the high
      summer pastures on Whinfell.
      This fold is shown as a pinfold on the 1867 OS 1:10,560 map and
      is still in use today albeit with wooden rails to enlarge the capacity.
      It is close to a stream coming from the
      fell and the pinfold probably originally
      served the purpose of impounding
      sheep and cattle illegally grazing on
      the common following the driving of
      Whinfell.
      Whinfell Common was enclosed in
      1828 and the map extract here shows
      the retention of the pinfold after
      enclosure.

P   Blindcrake pound. Grid ref: 314700,534700
Located in the corner of the village green, much altered and now
being used as a storage area containing a wooden shed. Structure
is shown but not named on the 1900 1:2,500 OS map. The water
source for the village and the impounded animals was a pond on
the green, now drained, not the stone troughs placed alongside

the nearby wall.
Blindcrake village
was designated a
conservation area
in 2001.
Horace Winter
in his *"A History
& Survey of
Blindcrake"*,
printed in 1987,
states that the
village green *"was
part of the Isel Estate, and previously the site of the village pond, called
the Mortar Dub, which was used for watering stock, and washing
horses legs after ploughing. It was blamed for recurring fevers in the
village, and after 1900, due mainly to the efforts of James Teasdale of
Millstone Moor, it was drained by Cockermouth Rural District Council,
in spite of strong opposition by local farmers. After this was done the
fevers subsided. The stone walled pound in the corner of the Green was
still used to impound stray stock."* (Kirkgate Centre, Cockermouth).
Recorded in the Manor Of Isel papers held at Carlisle Records
Office (CRO D/LAW/1/229) are two undated notes giving the two
decisions of the manor court which read: *John Carter of Blindcrake
& Henry Robert Brisco of Bothel for a pound-breach of the pound at
Blindcrake, according to pain 6s 8d.*
Wm Carter presents the pinfold at Blindcrake to be out of repaire.
No fine recorded.

C   Bolton pinfold. Grid ref: 363760,523170
This pinfold is not named on OS maps but the 1860 1:2500 and
1863 1:10,560 maps show a structure on the site. This is a large

almost square pinfold that was constructed by Andy Goldsworthy, on the site of the original village pinfold, as part of the five year public art, landscape and environment commission, managed and developed by Cumbria County Council. (1996-2002) It is one of a

series of 6 "Cone pinfolds" where a stone cone has been constructed in the centre of the fold as a public artwork.
It is approximately 11mtrs by 15mtrs with walls about 1.5mtrs high. The pinfold is constructed of various coloured sandstone and

capped with triangular red sandstone giving an overall impression of colour, light and space. The interior is grassed. The pinfold is now a piece of land art and is becoming part of the village heritage. There are plans to install a seat and erect an interpretation board. No written history is known. The parish council claimed legal ownership and purchased indemnity insurance prior to the rebuild by Andy Goldsworthy. Before its reconstruction locals described it as a "small semi-walled enclosure". There is no visible reason for its particular location away from any obvious source of water or manorial buildings. However the Ordnance Survey First Edition County Series map of 1863 shows a well at the site and a substantial dwelling named Elm House which may account for the pinfold being sited here.

S   Bothel pinfold. No trace. Grid ref: 318085,538620
This pinfold is shown on the 1867 OS 1:10,560 map but no trace now exits. Local information indicates that it was removed by Cumbria County Council in the 1950's.

S   Bowness-on-Windermere pinfold. No trace. Grid ref:
340540,497170. The 1862 OS 1:10,560 map shows the pinfold on the northern edge of the town but no trace could be found. The town has expanded considerably and the pinfold was probably lost as the large villas were built on Lake Road in the mid 1900s.

S   Braithwaite pinfold. No trace. Grid ref: 323026,523500.
This pinfold is shown but not named on the 1864 1:2,500 OS map but was not recorded on the revised map of 1868. It was sited on the village common and in 1818 it is recorded in manor court records that: "We the six jurors, request that the said township of Braithwaite and Coledale and Rogerside to put the Lordship's pinfould into good repair and every other thing that appertain to the said pinfould so that it may be reddy to put anything in that may encroach on the said Manners and Waste Ground"

The previous year the court set out the following to try to ensure that the Common was used as prescribed by the court. Any sheep found would have been impounded: "It is agreed by the above jurors that if any person have any tups that get a lamb going at large upon the Common in the Manor of Braithwaite and Coledale after the tenth day of October next and for every tup at large after that day we force him in a fine of one pound nineteen shillings and eleven pence. Each fine to be levied without further notice."

S   Brampton pinfold, Appleby. Site only. Grid Ref: 368233,523115

The site of the Brampton pinfold is opposite to Brampton Hall and shown on the 1863 OS 1:10,560 map. It's proximity to the "Manor House" and a marked well indicate that it is possibly the Manorial pinfold for the area.
When excavating the site for the foundations of the Village Hall, now built on the spot, a large stone believed to be a tether stone used in the pinfold was found and is now at the roadside.

S   Brampton pinfold, Carlisle. No trace. Grid ref: 353497,561193
The pinfold site on Fair Green is shown on the 1868 OS 1:10,560 map as a rectangular structure. According to Cumberland and

Westmorland Antiquarian and Archaeological Socieity (CWAAS) Vol LXXIII page 302 the police station now occupies the site of the old pinfold and tithe barn.

C   Brigham pound. Grid reference 309133,530006

This pound is named on the 1864 OS 1:2,500 and the 1867 OS 1:10,560 map. It is shown in open countryside on the banks of Ellerbeck, a tributary to the River Derwent. Although well preserved it may have been altered from its original shape, due to housing development, as the shape is irregular with one straight wall. It is approximately 16mtrs by 11mtrs with a modern gate. It was shown, in 1867, on the edge of common land with several tracks across it and the original ford through the beck is still in place but usefully supplemented by a bridge.

The pound is Grade II listed as follows:

Local authority reference number: NY 03 SE, Serial Number of entry in list: 4/82, Grade of building: II Civil Parish: Brigham, Allerdale, Village, address of building: Ellerbeck Brow (west side), Date when building was first listed: 3-3-67, Group value note: Cattle pound at High Ellerbeck Bridge, Cattle pound. Early C19. Calciferous sandstone rubble. Low dry stone wall with alternative large and small stone coping, enclosing a small roughly rectangular area between a field and the former road leading to a ford over the river. Now disused and overgrown but a rare survival in this area.

NF   Brisco pinfold. Grid reference 342232,551786

The only reference found is in the Transactions of the CWAAS New Series Vol XVII page 53 where it is recorded in court rolls in May 1715 that Pinner William Coates was appointed. No trace of the site could be found on maps or in the village although an area of common land on the south side of Brisco seems a likely site.

P   Brothybeck pinfold, Sebergham. Partial. Grid ref: 334247,542723.

Shown and named on the 1868 OS 1:10,560 map as a pinfold this location is unusual. It was, when visited, overgrown and in disrepair but the original footprint of the structure is clearly discernible. The 1868 map shows it close to a stream on a secondary track over Sebergham Common, which appears to be enclosed at this time and although not near a settlement, its isolated location on the map shows it is near a crossroads with an Inn, nearby mill and a tile maker.

C   Brough pinfold. (Church Brough) Grid ref: 79384,514214
       This is a circular pinfold constructed by Andy Goldsworthy, on the site of the village pinfold, as part of the five year public art, landscape and environment commission, managed and developed by Cumbria County Council. (1996-2002) It is located in the grounds of Church Brough school.

The original pinfold is shown and named on the 1859 OS 1:250,000 map and is on the edge of Coltsford Common close to the beck. The Monuments record Sites and Monuments Record 4227 notes that the surveyor could not locate it in 1996.

S   Brough Sowerby pinfold. Site only. Grid ref: 379770,512830.
       The site of this circular pinfold is now a grassed roadside area in Brough Sowerby. On the 1860 1:2,500 OS map it is shown outside Town Head farm at the edge of a small unfenced area in the centre of the hamlet.

NF   Burgh-by-Sands pinfold. No trace.
       A petition for the erection of a pinfold was signed by thirty six inhabitants of the Barony of Brugh (Burgh) in 1819 but no evidence of it being built in the Barony, consisting of Burgh, Aikton, Drumburgh and Westlinton, has been traced. The petition reads: Barony of Brugh. June 23rd 1819.
       "We the undersigned being Inhabitants of the Barony of Burgh having taken into consideration the Damages done to Inhabitants within the said Barony by People who turn out their Cattle, Horses etc. Into the High Roads and lanes within the said Barony whereby several trespasses have been committed upon the fields of

the Inhabitants adjoining the said Highways and lanes we therefore think it necessary to have a pinfold erected within the said Barony to prevent such trespass in future".

S   Burton in Kendal pinfold. Site only. Grid ref: 352870,476530
The site is shown on the 1862 OS 1:10,560 map as a rectangular structure. It was demolished to make way for ten council houses in 1948.

NF   Buttermere pound. No trace. The only record found for Buttermere was in the record of the court leet when on 16th October 1719 it was reported that the Turnmen of Buttermire presents the pound fold gate lyeing down and Amercie the inhabitants of the township 6s 8d.

C   Caldbeck – Potts Gill pinfold. Grid ref; 331845,537334.
This pinfold, not named on an OS map, nestles amongst farm buildings. It is a rectangular pinfold of random field stone with one wall built against a field bank. It is situated on the boundary between the fell land and cultivated fields and beside tracks that lead along the fell boundary  joining the small communities. A stream runs nearby. This pinfold has been restored and stabilised as part of the Sheepfolds project by Andy Goldsworthy. Its strategic position next to the fell indicates that it may have been specifically used to impound animals found illegally grazing on the fell.

P   Caldbeck – Townhead pound. Grid ref: 33195,539202.
This circular pinfold is shown on the 1863 1:2,500 OS map at the foot of Smithy Lane as it enters the hamlet of Townhead. Only part of the wall appears to be left and this forms part of a garden boundary.

S   Cark-in-Cartmel pound. Site only. Grid ref: 336629,476677.
A circular pinfold stood next to the river at Rosthwaite bridge Cark.

Shown on the 1890 1:2,500 ODS map and on the 1957 OS 6 inch map but now only an overgrown mound marks the site.

NF   Carleton pinfold. No trace.
Site could not be located on any OS map. The reference found was to a pinfold in Carleton in the Title Deeds of the Carlton Hall Estate held at Carlisle Records Office ref DCC2/23. The document refers to a piece of land bought by a John Birbeck in 1823 and "lying near the Place where the pinfold at Carleton aforesaid stood".

S   Carlisle – City pound. No trace. Grid ref: 34016,556498.
Shown on the 1746 map held at Carlisle RO. Site is now the Sands Centre.

NF   Carlisle – Newtown pinfold. No trace. Grid ref: 338920,556000.
Described as Newtown Animal pound on Sites and Monuments Record 10552 and sourced from the OS First Edition 6" Sheet No XX111.

NF   Carlisle Gate pinfold, Wigton. Grid Ref: 323855,541703 approx.
In 1780 it cost George O'Brien 5s to repair this pinfold and in 1929 it was in disrepair again. An approach was made to Lord Leconfield asking him to sell it to the landowner of an adjacent property. This sparked legal arguments around ownership and rights to keep stock in the pinfold. Cumbria Archive ref. SL/34. There is no trace of the pinfold on OS maps, local enquiries were negative and the site could not be traced.

P   Cartmel pound. Grid ref: 338033,478671.
This site is shown on the 1851 OS 1:2,500 map as a pound. Some parts of the original walls can be discerned but it now serves the purpose of a storage barn or garage. The water source is now culverted to allow for the modern driveway to an adjacent house. The site is recorded on the Cumbria Sites and  Monuments Record as SMR 16120. Locally the building is referred to as the roller house as it used to house a road roller.

NF   Casterton pinfold. No trace. Grid ref: 362461,479720.
      A small steep piece of river bank is known locally as the pinfold
      but not found named on any OS map. The 1898 and 1914 1:2,500
      OS maps show outlines of a plot next to the river but it is not
      named so no site can be confirmed.

NF   Clifton pinfold, Penrith. No trace. Although mentioned in the
      Westmorland Quarter Sessions papers ref. KRO/WQ/SR/273 the
      site could not be traced. The record reads "Presentment, Joseph
      Milner of Barton gent. And Dorothy Bowness of Clifton spinster,
      on 21 August 1757 broke into and entered the pinfold at Clifton
      and rescued one filly and one colt impounded by Margaret
      Robinson widow for doing damage to her ground. No bill".

S   Cockermouth pinfold. Grid ref: 312866,530807.
      The site is marked by a small copse of trees but there are no signs
      of the original rectangular pinfold shown on the 1866 OS Maps
      and Town Plan. The pinfold was at the south end of a large field
      named the Deer Orchard which may account for its location.

S   Colby pinfold, Appleby. No trace. Grid ref: 366730,52070.
      The site of this rectangular pinfold is shown on the 1861 1:2,500
      OS map and has now been replaced by a house named "Pinfold
      House".

S   Coldbeck pinfold, Ravenstonedale. Site not confirmed. Grid ref:
      372240,504350. The pinfold is marked on the 1859 1:2,500 OS
      map but road improvements and landscaping since then make it
      difficult to confirm the exact site. This may have been a paddock
      used as a pinfold. A small stone building may mark the site.

C   Crackenthorpe pinfold, Appleby. Grid
      ref: 66200,522200.
      Shown on the 1861 1:2,500 OS map
      as a pinfold with two small pools
      known as Gaylock Pools nearby.
      Cumbria Sites and Monuments
      Record Number 16749 updated
      1994.

This pinfold is approx.11mtrs by 10mtrs and in poor condition with one wall reduced to foundation stones only. There is evidence of several repair attempts over the years it has stood here on the edge of an access way to an old roman road.

NF Croasdale pinfold (also known as Crossdale).
The reference found is in Carlisle Records Office ref D/DI 1 and 9 where there are references to reduction in the width of road from "pinfold to the stone quarry" and a "Croasdale pinfold payment". No trace of a pinfold or quarry could found. Field patterns on the 1876 OS map indicate that this area was subject to the Enclosure Act and the pinfold may well have been removed as a result.

P Crook pinfold, Kendal. Grid ref: 346428,495109.
This is a restored pinfold, although the walls are much reduced in height, beside the road at Crook. It measures 20mtrs by 5mtrs and is close to the parish boundary. A spring in the far corner would have provided drinking water for the  stock. The 1860 1:2,500 OS map shows the pinfold placed on the roadway.

S Crook pound, Kendal (Pound Farm). Grid ref: 347065,495304
Shown and named on the 1860 1:2,500 OS map as an area of land with a large rectangular structure. In its isolated position it was probably used originally by drovers. It has several structures or buildings shown on this site but they appear to have been demolished when the farm developed as Pound Farm. Now a holiday lodge complex.

C Crosby Garrett pinfold. Grid ref: 372700,509243.
It is referred to locally as a pinfold and if it was it must have been the country's smallest. This very small circular structure is unlikely to have been a pinfold because of its small size, about 4 metres diameter. It also has a small outlet at ground level on its north side indicating that it may have been the site of a well. A local feature

is the marking of well sites with elaborate stone structures as in the nearby village of Soulby. It is not shown or named on early OS maps.

C   Crosby Ravensworth pinfold. Grid ref: 362102,514266.
     This pinfold site is shown on the1859 1:2,500 OS map and was re-constructed by Andy Goldsworthy, on the site, as part of the

five year public art, landscape and environment commission, managed and developed by Cumbria County Council (1996-2002). It is one of a series of six "cone pinfolds" where a stone cone has been constructed in the centre of the fold as a public artwork.

NF   Crosby pinfold, Maryport. Site not identified.
     Information received indicated a pinfold in the grounds of Westlands Farm but no trace found. Not found on any OS maps.

P   Crosthwaite Pinfold Hill, Lyth.   Grid ref: 346230,488319.
     This is a large roughly circular hedge pinfold shown on the 1896 1:2,500 OS map as Pinfold Hill. It is in poor condition with very little of the stone walling, possibly an original feature, left. The walling would have supported the hawthorn hedge that surrounds the site. The interior is as

its name suggests higher than the surrounding land. This pinfold would have been built specifically at this spot because of the rocky outcrop at its centre. Around this large outcrop the land is higher, as a result of the deposits caused by receding ice when the valley was formed

Before the valley was drained the pinfold would have been the only dry spot in this part of the valley and a refuge for grazing cows and sheep. It is said that "pinnell" was quarried from within the pinfold. Pinnell is a mixture of small rock and sand deposited naturally as the valley formed and was ideal hardcore for surfacing the local roads and tracks. The Parish Records show that as a result of the Enclosure Award of 1815, the pinfold, known as Low Gate Quarry after the nearby Low Gate Farm, was transferred to the care of the parish council. It is currently let at a minimal rent.

P   Culgaith pinfold, Penrith. Grid ref: 361062,529706.
This is another pinfold partly demolished since 1900 for road

widening, however what is left is kept in good order. It is shown but not named on OS maps including the 1900 1:2,500 OS map. Interestingly its location at a crossroads in the  village is significant in that old paths from enclosed land converge to the pinfold and nearby were the smithy, institute, church and more recently the war memorial. Another indication of the pinfold's status in this village is that it is registered on the Common Land Register as CL439.

C   Dalston pound, Carlisle. Grid ref;
337147,549042.
A small triangular pinfold at the south end of the village of Dalston. In good condition with one side bordering the River Caldrew. Approx. 7m by 20 m. It is registered by Dalston Parish Council as Common Land CL 332.

C   Dalton-in-Furness pound. Grid ref: 322645,473812.
     An ancient pound at Goose Green which is approx. 11mtrs in
     diameter with a modern metal
     gate. It is shown on numerous
     maps the clearest of which is
     the Merryweather town plan
     of Dalton surveyed in 1825.
     It is Grade II listed and even
     mentioned in an account of
     the Civil War when in 1643
     the crews from a small fleet of
     Parliamentary ships anchored

     at Piel Harbour joined locals and advanced on Dalton the men
     occupying the pinfold in their attack.

S   Dalton-in-Kendal pound. Grid ref: 354227,476812
     This site is possibly a pre-medieval village pound according to
     Tom Clare in his book Archaeological Sites of The Lake District.
     It consists of a broken circle of oval limestone boulders. It is a
     registered archaeological site and mentioned here for reference only.

NF   Dean. Site not found. Grid ref: 307500,525247
     Information received that there was a pound in Dean but no
     evidence found.

S   Deanscales pinfold. Partial. Grid ref: 309438,526326.
     This site, with possibly two original walls now the field boundary, is
     in the corner of a piece of common land on the far side of a beck.
     It is shown on the 1867 1:10,560 OS map.

P   Dearham pinfold, Maryport. Grid REF: 307126,536294.
     This corner pinfold is now much
     encroached upon by modern housing
     even since it was recorded on the 1889
     1:2,550 OS map. Later maps show
     the progress of this encroachment up
     until the house, named pinfold, was
     built around 1960. The lane beside the

pinfold leads to Dearham Park which is now enclosed fields and around the village boundaries are signs of strip field farming and enclosed fields indicating the importance of a pinfold in this ancient village.

S   Dent pinfold. Grid ref: 371590,483280.
The 1853 OS 1:10,560 shows and names a pinfold at this reference but forty years later the 1893 OS 1:2,500 map names it as a sheepfold. As the site is on the fell side far from a settlement it is unlikely to be a pinfold in terms of the definition used in this study. Noted here for reference purposes.

C   Eaglesfield pound, Cockermouth.
Grid ref: 309510,528217.
This is a small pound built between a steep bank and a stream on the edge of the village. It is not named but the structure is outlined on the 1881 1:2,500 OS map. The parish council repaired the walls and planted an oak tree to mark the 2000 millennium.

C   Edenhall pinfold, Penrith.Grid ref: 356567,532622.
Although marked and named on all early OS maps as a sheepfold it has the hallmarks of a being a pinfold. It is at the edge of a strip of "common land", it has high walls and is beside a track leading to Langwathby Moor. There is however no obvious water source.
The parish council have ownership and they rent it out, at a nominal amount, to a villager for use as a garden.

S Egremont pinfold. Grid ref: 301202,510700

The pinfold is marked on the 1872 1:2,500 OS map as in Lamb Lane but site today has modern housing built on it. No trace remains. A pinfold was in existence in 1677* as the Borough Court of Egremont records that John Skaif was presented for rescuing several sheep from the Borough pinfold as they were being driven

to it and notes that he was fined 8s 4d. Another entry for October 17th 1681 records that the pinfold "was broken down and cast downe every yeare by evil persons who kept unlawful goods to the great loss and damage of the town and burrough. We therefore , the said jurie for the public good of our town and burrough doe give and grant on behalf of the old town and burrow aforesaid to our well beloved friend and Burrowman, John Williamson of Egremont, Batchelor, two pieces of Burrow common wastes or mesne ground called Low Ridding Nooke, and Greenthwaite Nooke, which adjoin the said John Williamsons ground, containing one acre, or thereabouts, to him, for ever, for and in consideration of building a common pinfold two yards high in wall, and as large in compass as the said now hedged pinfold doth contain, within one year, more or less, he the said John Williamson assigns paying unto the Lord the fee thereof the annual quit rent of one penny".

The court did not stop there with their instructions about the pinfold: "And further we the said jury do order that the said John Williamson doe build the said common pinfold near to the pinfold now....before the first day of May next with hewn stone, door cheekes in the same, and the water to run the said pinfold".

Demonstrating that there were usually several pinfolds in a township one such site in Egremont was given away to Isaac Pearson in 1710 on condition that he repaired Skitterbeck bridge. Later entries show Joseph Head appointed pinfold Keeper in 1868, James Marshall in 1871 and a problem with the water running to the pinfold in 1876. This was recorded as "Mr Porter complains that the ancient water course which used to run through the pinfold has been obstructed or diverted and proposes that a Committee be appointed to examine into the matter; we having considered his complaint do appoint Mr Porter, Mr Coulthard, and Mr Iredale, and the hedge and ditch lookers to be a Committee for the purpose, and we enjoin the Committee to report to the Steward within one month from this date, and if the complaint is reported to be well founded, we request the steward to take such steps as may be necessary on behalf of the Lord of the Manor to have it remedied"

A series of letters dated April 1902** refer to pinfold repairs. Messrs Davidson of Lowther Street Whitehaven wrote to Mr W Banks at Lowther Castle advising him that a "portion of the wall on the south side of the pinfold has fallen. A new door is also required as the old one is completely done. The cost of repairing the wall would be 28 shillings and a new door with lock say 12 shillings". Mr Banks sought permission to carry out the repairs from the manorial landowner pointing out that mineral rights for the site are owned by the Wythop Mining Company so would he "kindly give the necessary instructions to have the work done as little acts of ownership are often found useful". Clearly trying to safeguard ownership of the site should minerals of value be found. Permission was given on 25th April 1902 and instructions issued accordingly.

*Transactions of the CWAAS Vol XVII pp 69-71

**Whithaven Records Office D/LEC 280/21

C   Embleton pinfold. Grid ref: 316264,529406.

I was informed about this unusual pinfold by a local parish councillor who has known this building to be called the pinfold for over 50 years. The open structure attached to the lean-to is the pinfold. It was roofed up to about 20 years ago and belongs to St Cuthbert's Church in whose grounds it stands. The adjoining building is the meeting room and storage room for the church.

It is not named on the OS maps but is shown on the 1864 1:2,500 OS map as an open structure.

C   Field Broughton pound. Grid ref:
338531,481606.

A well maintained pound on White Moss Common, listed as "Oval plan enclosure approx. 8mtrs by 11mtrs with wall approx 2mtrs high". Parish council records show that the pound was used for storage and also had to be cleared of rubbish on several occasions. It has been regularly repaired, most recently in 2004 when with the aid of Lottery funding it was restored to its current condition.

S   Gaitsgill pinfold, (Gatesgill) Carlisle. Site only. Grid ref: 338796,546759

The site of this pinfold is subsumed into the private garden of Bridge House formerly Pinfold House and is not accessible. Shown but not named on OS maps it is also registered on the Common Land Register, CL 331.

C   Garsdale pinfold, Sedburgh. Grid ref: 374912,489648.

Situated at pinfold Farm in Garsdale is a fold recorded on the 1852 1:2,500 OS map and which gives its name to the area and to the roadside cottages of Pinfold House, Pinfold Farm and West Pinfold (now Rose Cottage). It is a small fold that was until recently used to rear geese and now contains a garden shed.

S   Gleaston, Ulverston. Grid ref: 325832,470750.

Although included here this fold is probably a sheepfold or washfold. It is on the bank of a stream with two entrances. OS maps which show the area of common in Gleaston to have had several sheepwashes and shows this one as a sheepfold on the 1889 1:2,500 OS map although locally it has been called a pinfold.

S   Grange-over-Sands pound. Grid ref: 340413,478119.

Shown as a pound on the 1860 OS 1:10,560 map. The site now has a preserved well known as Charney Well but no trace of the pound. Housing development around the site prevents its accurate location being identified.

NF   Grasmere. No trace.

The early OS maps show only sheepfolds. However in the sixteenth century Grasmere boasted three folds used as pinfolds. Two were for stock straying from manors of Wythburn, (to the north) and Rydal (to the south), and one for strays belonging to the tenants of Grasmere. In the 1847 Rate Book for Grasmere it is recorded that the pinfold belonging to the Parish was falling into disrepair.**

*The Harvest of the Hills by Angus Winchester p 117.

** CWAAS Transactions Vol XXVIII page 288

S   Great Asby pound , Appleby. Site only. Grid ref: 368306,513340.

Outline only shown on OS maps. A local source confirms that this pound was demolished circa 2000 and the stone used for a boundary wall next to Asby Hall. This was a registered monument SMR 15268 and was visited in 1996 by the surveyor who described it as "a small rectangular enclosure of stone with no entrance other than a small narrow gap, located on the north-east edge of Gt Asby village".

P   Great Asby – Butts Green pinfold, Appleby. Grid ref: 368186,313500.

The pinfold is shown on the 1859 1:2,500 OS map next to a stream feeding Asby Beck and alongside a track to the open fell.

The only remaining signs of this rectangular pinfold are the two limestone gate posts. Having the two pinfolds in Great Asby is unusual.

One may have replaced the other as the village grew or as is often referred to in manorial records one could have been the common pound and the other the manorial pound.

C   Great Broughton pinfold, Cockermouth. Grid ref: 307432,531634. The Great Broughton Parish records for 12th October 1793 state that there was a need for the "maintenance of pinfold door and

cheeks" of this pinfold. On 23rd March 1886 a Mr Paisley the owner of an adjacent property was offered purchase of this pinfold by the overseer. As a result he contacted Mr S.G.Saul in Lord Leconfield's office at Cockermouth Castle who

questioned whether it could be sold as it was now the responsibility of the Highways Board of Cockermouth. The outcome is not recorded but today it is rented from the council, is complete and well used as a private domestic garden. It is shown on the 1895 1:2,500 OS map.

NF   Great Musgrave pound. Grid ref: 376800,513500
The Cumbria Sites and Monuments record, entry SMR 4119 describes this site "at west end of village is a sub-rectangular enclosure, later used as a pound, but probably of earlier origin. The bank survives on the south-west side up to 2.5m high". It is believed to be a medieval earthwork and as in the case of Dalton-in-Kendal is noted here for reference only.

C   Great Strickland pinfold, Penrith. Grid ref: 356150,522999. This low walled pinfold is complete and maintained well. It is approximately 5mtrs by 6mtrs and is named on the 1898 1:2,500 OS map. The entrance is too narrow and the walls too low for

effective animal use and may be the result of consolidation work after it fell into disuse.
Although maintained by the parish council they do not own it. A modern house has been built immediately behind the pinfold named Sycamore House, presumably

after the fifty year old tree in the pinfold rather than the over 200 year old pinfold!

S   Grayson Green pinfold. Site only. Grid ref: 299787,524822
Shown on the 1900 1:2,500 OS map as "old pinfold" it has now disappeared. The corner of the field where the pinfold was located also had a well which has likely been neglected and the site is now very swampy. A modern housing development makes close access to the site impossible.

C   Greysouthern pinfold. Grid ref: 307194,529342.
This large oval pinfold has been much modified over the years and is now a village amenity. The latest alterations happened at the millennium when it was made into a play and seating area for the community. A plaque commemorates the opening in June 2001.

The 1866 1:2,500 OS map shows this pinfold in a typical location for an early pinfold, near a well and just off the central open area in the village on the edge of open farmland.

C   Hardbank pinfold, Warwick Bridge.
Grid ref: 35200,556780.
Shown on the 1863 1:2,500 OS map this pinfold is complete but shows the signs of changes over the years to allow access to neighbouring properties.

C   Hartley pinfold, Kirkby Stephen. Grid ref: 378280,508895.
An irregular shaped, allegedly heart shaped to reflect the name of the village (sic) pinfold. It is shown on the 1859 1:2,500 OS map and stands on a piece of common land beside the stream. It is of mainly dry stone wall construction with a modern wooden gate.
In 1957 it became Grade II listed and is described as "on the

village green, possibly late C18 with rough dressed gate posts, trapezoid in plan with C20 wooden gate to the centre of the side facing street"

As a result of the Commons Registration Act of 1965 the pinfold and land on which it stood had no registered owner so in 1979 the Commons Commissioner opened a hearing to decide on ownership. He heard evidence from the Parish Meeting Chairman and Clerk that the Parish Meeting had always maintained the land and pinfold and that no-one had ever laid claim to ownership. On 22nd July 1980 the Commissioner declared that he was satisfied that the Parish Meeting are the reputed owners of the land and pinfold. The submission describes the history of the pinfold as derived from documentation and local people's memory and is typical of the life of a pinfold once its real purpose was no longer needed.

NF   Hawcoat pound, Barrow-in-Furness. Grid ref: 320300,471920
The site of a pound is recorded on the Cumbria Sites and Monuments Record SMR 2291 where it is noted that in Richardson's Furness Past & Present "an ancient pinfold, now a garden in the centre of the village of Hawcoat, was the scene of a smart skirmish between Royalists and Parliamentarians in 1643". This site could not be found.

S   High Hesket pinfold. Grid ref: 347990,543630.
Site shown on the OS 1863 1:2,500 map but site is now a bungalow.

S   High Ireby pinfold. Grid re: 323038,537067.
Site shown on 1867 1:10,560 OS map but no trace left.

C   Hilton pinfold, Appleby. Grid ref: 373240,520630.
This pinfold is close to Hilton Hall bordering the village green with a water trough nearby. It is shown but not named on the 1861 1:2,500 OS maps and later ones.

P   Hunsonby pinfold, Penrith. Grid ref: 358026,535500

This pinfold is shown on the 1867 OS 1:10,560 maps. Only a part of the wall is still in existence but the circular outline can be traced. It is in a picturesque setting next to a stream on the edge of the village.

P   Hutton Roof pinfold, Kirkby Lonsdale. Grid ref: 356960, 477820.
This site is shown on the 1862 1:10,560 OS map. Just the outline of this pinfold remains which shows it be about 10mtrs by 12mtrs with a stream alongside.

NF   Ireleth. No trace. Grid ref: 321983,477592.
In main street is Pinfold House but no trace of a pinfold. The area is built up and the 1890 1:2,500 OS map does not show a pinfold.

NF   Isel Old Park pinfold. No trace.
There is a reference to Isel Old Park pinfold in the manorial records Court Roll for the Manor of Isel 1660-1712 at Cumbria Records Office ref D LAW /2/6 but location could not be found.

S   Kendal – Ferney Green pinfold. Grid ref: 351113,493353.
This pinfold is shown on the 1860 OS Town Plan of Kendal but by the 1898 1:2,500 OS map Kendal Green had been developed and it was not shown. Site is now an open space.

C   Kentmere. Grid ref: 345790,504092.
An irregularly shaped pinfold is shown on the 1860 1:2,500 OS map but it has since been altered to allow access to a nearby property. It is referred to in a book by Len Hayton "The collected tales of a Lakeland Lad" where he writes "my grandfather always referred to the stretch of road from Low Bridge House to the bottom of Church Hill as the Pumple Syke,

his pronunciation of Pinfald Syke. The Kentmere village pound was situated just outside the gate to Pumple Syke. It was a boggy place with a stream flowing through it which never seemed to dry up in a drought". Restored in 2000.

P Kirkandrews-upon-Eden pinfold, Carlisle. Grid ref: 335374,558394.

This is a triangular site shown on the 1867 1:2,500 OS map as "Green" and later on the 1971 1:2,500 OS map as "The Common" but never as the pinfold. The parish council maintain the area and refer to it as the pinfold. It is not possible to see how this was a pinfold as the area's use has obviously changed its appearance over the years.

S Kirkby Lonsdale Fellside. Grid ref: 359285,479419.

This fold is a bit ambiguous as it is shown but not named on the 1859 OS map and from 1898 is named as a sheepfold. Close examination shows the building has been much amended and appears to have two entrances. It is next to a stream and on the 1914 OS map there are two structures named as a sheepwash and sheepfold. It is unlikely to have been a pinfold and is recorded here for interest.

S Kirkby Stephen pound. Grid ref: 376750,509350.

The Cumbria Sites and Monuments Record 16914 suggests this may have been an animal pound but it is not named as such on OS maps although later OS maps show a building near the actual site. The location is now a pile of rubble not discernible as a pinfold.

C Kirkby Thore pinfold, Appleby-in-Westmorland. Grid ref: 363840,525753.

This pinfold is Grade II listed. Described as "Village pound, probably late C18. Rectangular enclosure has 5ft high coursed, squared, rubble walls with triangular coping stones; C20 gate in east wall. Late 19c building to rear originally served as school lavatory before becoming the fire-engine house; now disused. Squared snecked rubble with quoins. Welsh slate roof. Single storey, built at right angles to road with door in end wall." This is a rectangular structure that appears to have been extended since its original construction probably at the time the small roofed building was added. At the time of the first visit in April 2004 it was in good condition and used for storage. In July 2004 the wall to the right of the gated entrance had been demolished and a tractor was parked within the pinfold. The pinfold is shown on the First Edition County Series of the Ordnance Survey map for 1863. Parish council records first mention the pinfold in April 1896 when it was proposed that the village fire hose be kept in it. In 1896 it was agreed that the door to the fire hose house be altered to permit the entrance of the new fire hose cart. In August 1950 the parish council considered conversion of the pinfold building to a garage, at a cost of £49, to rent out but in March 1951 this scheme was dropped with no reason recorded. The pinfold was used to store a ladder during 1978 as the records show that the "street lighting attendant" was repeatedly asked to return the council ladder to the pinfold. In 1988 the pinfold was rented out for £100 per year but the records show that notice was given for the tenant to vacate in 1991. It was then used to store play equipment for the Mother and Toddler group from 1997 until 1998. In October 1998 consideration was given to convert to public toilets but this idea was not pursued.

In 1999 interest in buying the pinfold was expressed by the owner of a neighbouring property and this raised the issue of legal ownership. This was eventually resolved and the pinfold was sold by the parish council in 2003. This history was provided by Kirkby Thore PC.

S   Kirkoswald pinfold, Penrith. Grid ref: 355601,541129
     Clearly shown on the 1888 1:2,500 OS map but it had disappeared from the map and replaced by a Smithy on the 1900 1,2500 OS map. Since then garage buildings have been built on the site. It cannot be confirmed but some stonework at the end of the buildings still remains which may be part of the pinfold.

P   Lamplugh – Bird Dyke pinfold. Grid ref: 309078,521358
     Shown as a pinfold on the 1895 1:2,500 OS map at the foot of a track to the open fell. Later maps show the house built next to it and a diversion in this track. pinfold is now overgrown and in derelict condition.

S   Lazonby pinfold. Grid ref: 354710,539590.
     Shown on the 1863 1:2,500 OS map as next to a smithy but not shown on the 1900 OS map. Location is now an industrial site with housing and although access could not be gained it seems unlikely that it still exists.

S   Levens pinfold. Grid ref: 348603,486764.
     The site has been identified but no trace of the pinfold now exists. It is believed that the pinfold was lost when after the Heversham Enclosure Act of 1805 the allotment of the commons, including the area of the pinfold, was made to a William Addison. Indentures in 1817 and 1837 refer to the sale of pinfold Lot and Pinfield Lot respectively. On 13th February 1876 a codicil to the will of John Pennie was proven and a freehold close of land called Pinfold Parrock in the occupation of Edward Dodd Kemp as tenant was sold.
     The Levens Highway Book 1810 to 1850 records the work required and carried out to maintain the roads around Levens. It has an entry dated February 26th 1811 which reads: "from Cinderbarrow

to Pinfold from thence to Pinfold. Rob.t Philipsons. 18ft wide 1174 roods at 4/-. £23.10.1 ".

Although the meaning of this entry is unclear the Highway Book contains many references to "breaking stones" for repair to roads and this is believed to be a description of the work needed.

A letter undated and enclosed in the pages of the book from H. Ellison to Mr Spicer , Surveyor of Roads, Levens reads " Sir, You being the surveyor of the Roads in Levens Township I wish without Delay you would have the pinfold put in Order and call a meeting to appoint a person to take up Cattle turned into the lanes there – I have had considerable damage done by Dobsons Cows amongst my potatoes and certainly you as Surveyor ought not to suffer Cattle to go in the roads. I am Sir Your Obdt Servant." Ref KRO WDX 809.

C   Little Broughton pinfold. Grid ref: 307851,531858.
This is a well preserved pinfold situated beside the old village green in Little Broughton and shown clearly on the 1886 1:2,500 OS map. It is owned by the parish council and leased to the owners of Birchless House who use it as a garden.

In the manorial records held at Carlisle Records Office there is reference to the repair to the "pinfold door and cheeks" dated 12th October 1793.

NF   Little Langdale, pinfold How Bridge.
An indication that a pinfold may have existed, is in the name of this bridge in Little Langdale. Reference to this bridge being in decay is held in KRO WQ/SR/509. However it could not be found. It is included here for reference only.

S   Little Musgrave pinfold. Grid ref: 376040,513130
The 1898 OS 1:2,500 map shows the pinfold but local information is that about 10 years ago the site was cleared and a new cottage, Pinfold Cottage, was built in its place.

C Longtown pinfold, Carlisle. (C)
Grid ref: 337686,568934.
Clearly shown as a two celled
pinfold on the 1895 1:2,500 and
the 1868 1:10,560 OS maps as a
standing beside the road north of
the bridge in Longtown. However
the 1901 OS map indicates

changes to the road to the north of the bridge and the bridge
itself but the pinfold is not shown. I suspect therefore that the
pinfold is a modern build near the original site. It is well kept and
approximately 2.5mtrs square.

S Lorton pound, Cockermouth. Grid ref: 316133,525481.
Traditionally the area of common
land at the rear of the old brewery
building in High Lorton is known
as the poundfold. A circular
structure is shown on the survey
map for the enclosures made in
1827 but was not on later OS maps.
An early reference to the function of

the pound as it related to grazing rights in the Lorton fells comes as
early as 1474 when the Brackenthwaite Court deemed that " Lorton
Heders to be inclosed and kept inclosed during the open season and
there the neighbours stray cattle may be driven".
The Parliamentary Survey of 1649 uses the poundfold as a
boundary reference "and soe along Peals of the Tenters westwards to
the poundfold and so over white Beck to John Wilkinsons".

C Loweswater pinfold. Grid ref: 312912,521765.
This isolated pinfold on the banks
of Loweswater served a very rural
community. It is built near the head of
the valley at a point between the open
fell and improved grazing at the valley
head. It is shown on the 1863 1:2,500
OS map and is maintained by LDNP.

In the Manorial Records of Sir Wilfred Lawson, Baron, there is recorded in 1749 "We find stocks and pounfold in good repair" and even earlier in 1674 it is recorded "By examination of the constables find ye stock and poundfold to be in sufficient repair". This is an unusual entry and in contrast to most manor court records that only record the condition of the pinfold if it is need of repair.

The extract here is from the Darling Fell enclosure map of 1865 showing the pinfold beside the Mosser Highway which ran alongside Lowesewater.

NF Melmerby pound. No trace. Grid ref: 361440,537300
Cumbria Sites and Monuments Record number 5860 records a circular earthwork as a cockpit or the remains of the village pound. The village also has a sheep washfold restored in 2001. There was and poundbreak in 1863 but this is not confirmed.

S Middleton pinfold. Grid ref: 362536,487332. Shown on 1859 1:2,500 map and later maps but farm development appears to have seen the end of this pinfold.

S Milnthorpe pinfold. Grid ref: 349630,461810.
Shown on the 1858 1:2,500 OS map but no trace now left due to development of the land. It is mentioned in the plaque at the entrance to Grisleymire Lane.

C Mungrisdale pound.
Grid ref: 336446,530014.
Shown on the 1899 1:2,500 OS map and now used as a wild flower garden. One wall has been replaced with a hedge due to road widening.

NF   Nateby pinfold, Kirkby Stephen.
Grid ref: 377480,506840.
Shown on the 1859 1:2500 OS map but now no trace could be found. New houses and road widening probably caused its demise.

S   Newbiggin pinfold, Appleby.
Grid ref: 363050,528640.
Site found but no trace of pinfold left. Roadside improvements with new walling probably caused its demise.

S   Newbiggin pinfold, Penrith. Grid ref: 347090,529120.
Shown as a sheepfold on the 1864 1:2,500 OS map however the conveyance dated 1910 refers to the site as a pinfold and confirms that the jury agrees that Mr Hodgson takes the pinfold agreeing to do the walling himself.

C   Newton Reigny, Penrith. Grid ref: 348114,531484.
This pinfold is on the edge of the village of Newton Reigny and has been adapted to use as a garden and storage area. A field gate has breached the walls but it is otherwise complete. Shown on various OS over the years as a pinfold and sheepfold.

S   Orton pinfold. Grid ref: 362400,508300.
Cumbria Sites and Monuments Record number 15196 refers to the site of this pinfold. In April 1986 it is recorded in the SMR that the minutes of the Court Baron of the Manor of Orton of 17 May 1843 refer to an application by John Simpson to build a house and smithy on the south side of Orton pinfold. The application was granted. Around the turn of the century the smithy and house were known as Derby House. Sometime later it was modernised and is now known as Shallowford. A few yards north of Shallowford is the Methodist chapel, built in 1833. The pinfold would therefore appear to have been situated between the old house and smithy, and the chapel. No traces remain today".

S Oulton pinfold, Wigton Grid ref: 324440,551610.
A house used as a Poor House was built on the site in 1825 and only the wall of the original large pinfold is left.

C Outgate pound, Hawkshead. Grid ref: 335520,499872.

A banked pinfold which has suffered changes due to road improvements and is recorded as a pound on the 1890 1:2,500 OS map. It is Grade II listed recorded on 15.3.1970 as "pound. Possibly C18 or earlier in origin. Stone rubble. Roughly rectangular enclosure, wall to street is approx. 13.5m long, low, with concrete coping and iron rails: post box in pier next to small gate. South wall is similar, north and west walls higher".
The parish council suggest that Lord Buccleuch owns the pinfold and that local landowners are responsible for its upkeep.

C Outhgill pinfold, Kirkby Stephen. Grid ref: 378386,501566.
The 1859 and 1915 1:2,500OS maps both show this pinfold as

originally circular but since then it has been partly reclaimed to allow a building and garden to develop. The cone inside is by Andy Goldsworthy, as part of the five year public art, landscape and environment commission, managed and developed by Cumbria County Council (1996-2002). It is one of a series of six "cone pinfolds" where a stone cone has been constructed in the centre of the fold as a public artwork.

S Papcastle pinfold. Grid ref: 311089,531536.
This is shown as a square pinfold in a small copse on the 1900 1:2,500 OS map but now the site has various houses built on it. A reference found in Whitehaven Records Office ref D/LEC 299 roll 19/20 refers to the Papcastle Court held on 10th October in the 23rd year of the reign of Henry VIII (1533) reads: " they present

Thomas Lamplughtt of Doven (a village just north of Papcastle) by his servant for 1 foldbreach (fined 40d) and for 12 pigs (2s) 16 sheep and 30 geese on the cow pasture of the neighbourhood at the several season".

C   Penruddock pinfold.
Grid ref: 342798,527723.
This pinfold is combined with a well has a nearby stream which makes the area boggy. Access is via a short wide track. It is in an open field area between the two settlements that make up

the township. It is now owned by the parish council who maintain it.

S   Plantation Bridge pinfold, Kendal. Grid ref; 348480,496600.
Shown as triangular and utilising the dry stone walls in the corner of a field. This site of this pinfold is on the 1860 1:2,500 OS map and close to Burrow Hall.

C   Pooley Bridge pinfold.
Grid ref: 347556,524486.
A pinfold that is maintained by the Lake District National Park with a seat to encourage its use! Although the dry stone walls are diminished in height and prone to disrepair this pinfold has stood on this

site close to Mainshouse, now Manor Farm, since before 1861. It is next to a stream and on the edge of open moorland.

S   Quality Corner pinfold, Whitehaven. Grid ref: 299176,519709.
Named on the 1867 1:10,560 OS map and shown as an irregular square shape in a field corner. Only a pile of stones now remain at the site.

C   Raisbeck pinfold, Orton. Grid ref: 364740,507120. The OS 1:2,500 maps name this structure as a sheepfold in 1857 and from 1914 a pinfold. The change in name seems to have occurred at the same time as the Raise Beck ceased to  become a ford and was bridged by the appropriately named Pinfold Bridge. The cone inside is by Andy Goldsworthy, as part of the five year public art, landscape and environment commission, managed and developed by Cumbria County Council (1996-2002). It is one of a series of six "cone pinfolds" where a stone cone has been constructed in the centre of the fold as a public artwork.

S   Red Dial pinfold, Wigton. Grid ref: 325824,546094. This pinfold, of which there is now no sign, stood on a patch of waste or common land and was shown on the OS maps dated 1867 and 1900 but had disappeared by the 1925 version.

S   Redmain pinfold, Blindcrake. Grid ref: 313660,533800. No trace found of this pinfold which is shown on the 1865 1:2,500 OS map.

S   Renwick pound, Penrith. Grid ref: 359500,543500. This is a small area of ground that is locally called the pound and believed to have been the place used to corral animals when there was a threat to the village from wild animals or raiding reivers. It is an irregular shaped piece of ground at the rear of several houses and has only narrow entrances and exits making it easy to block or defend. Listed here for reference purposes.

S   Rosley pinfold, Penrith. Grid ref: 331814,545617. The fairground at Rosley became a natural meeting point for travellers and drovers from the Solway plain in the north and the Scottish borders beyond. It was an open space of some forty acres

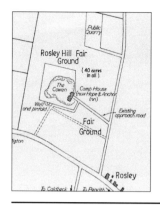

and is shown on the 1824 Enclosure Plan for Westward Parish. The pinfold is shown on the plan and would have served to impound stray cattle and horses during the fair. A well was in the centre of the pinfold and probably this accounts for its location.

The pinfold is shown but not named on the 1893 OS map but is named on the 1900 1:2,500 OS map. There is now no trace of the pinfold.

S   Roundthwaite pinfold, Tebay. Grid ref: 360920,503300.
No trace is now left of this pinfold is shown on the 1881 1:2,500 OS map on the edge of the village at the conversion of several ancient tracks coming in from Roundthwaite Common. It had disappeared by the time the OS surveyor for the area made his 1898 version.

NF   Sadgill, Longsleddale.
There are several large folds named as sheepfolds near the small settlement of Sadgill at the head of Longsleddale on the early 1:2,500 scale OS maps. Angus Winchester in his book "The Harvest of the Hills" refers to two pinfolds at Sadgill in the sixteenth century built by two owners of the dalehead, so that each could impound the other's stock. These may be the folds marked as they appear to be on private land away from the public road.

S   Scales pinfold, Ulverston. Grid ref: 327490,472270.
An area at Scales Green is known as the pinfold and the 1891 1:2,500 OS map shows a circular structure in this area. It was not shown on the 1968 map. The area is still known locally as the pinfold and is used as a childrens playground and private garden from which the parish council receives an income.

S   Seaton pinfold, Workington. Grid ref: 301990,530350.
Pinfold and trough shown on the 1866 OS 1:2,500 map but this site is now built upon and no trace of pinfold was found.

C   Sedburgh pinfold.
     Grid ref: 366672,491951.
     This is well preserved example of a
     pinfold shown on the 1894 1:2,500
     OS map as a pound. However on
     the 1909 and the 1970 map it is
     marked but not named although the

nearby caravan site is named Pinfold Caravan Site. This pinfold is
well kept and unusually appears to have two gateways!

P   Setmurthy pinfold.
     Grid ref: 318482, 532310.
     The 1866 1:2,500 OS map shows
     the irregularly shaped pinfold at the
     road junction north of the church.
     Part of a wall is all that remains.
     The pinfold and the strip of land
     adjacent to a beck on which it stood

was sold for 5s in 1891 to the local cleric who already had shooting
rights over the land. However as was the practice the rights to
extract any minerals from the site was retained by the Lord of the
Manor, Baron Leconfield.

NF   Skelton.
     There are references in the Carlton Cowper family records held at
     Carlisle Records Office to a pinfold in Skelton in 1790 reference D/
     CC/1. However OS maps do not show the pinfold and on a visit
     to the village no site was located.

S   Skirwith pinfold. Grid ref: 361750,532650.
     The 1867 1:2,500 OS map shows a circular pinfold beside the
     river but no trace now exists. The papers of the Hudleston family
     are held in the Records Office under ref: DHUD/9/2/4 and record
     an unusual use of the Skirwith pinfold in October 1751: "Thomas
     Birkbeck as inspector to watch the border with Westmorland, to
     prevent movement of cattle from there, where the infection now
     rages, was on watch today at about 10 or 11 am saw two persons
     driving 17 cattle into Cumberland, on Culgaith Moor he challenged

them, they ignored him, and drove them on into Skirwith; he roused the district, and when they got no further than Skirwith pinfold, wherein the cattle now are; he then rode to Hutton John to make this statement: adds that he hears one of the men is Thomas Taylor of Penton; the other behaved as if his servant".

S   Sockbridge pinfold, Penrith. Grid ref: 350136,526807.
Accessible only by footpath alongside Lady Beck to the rear of the garden of Pinfold House, Sockbridge. Structure is named as Sheepfold on the 1859 1:2,500 OS map and unnamed on later maps. Only a small part of one wall can be identified.

S   Soulby pinfold, Kirkby Stephen. No trace. Grid ref: 374884,511049.
The pinfold once stood in the centre of the village and is recorded on the 1859 & 1925 1:2,500 OS map. A local source believes it was removed in the 1960's.

S   Sour Nook pinfold, Temple Sowerby. No trace. Grid ref: 337090,540810.
Field corner is fenced off and has a stream but there is no trace of the pinfold named on the 1862 1:2,500 OS map.

C   St Bees pinfold.
Grid ref: 297184,511606.
A well preserved pinfold shown on the 1864 1:2,500OS map where it is on a track leading to open fell. It is now next to a builder's yard and at the side of a road which has led to one wall apparently being demolished and rebuilt after 1864. It is on the Common Land Register number CL219.

S   Staffield pinfold, Kirkoswald. Grid Ref: 354410,542900.
Shown on the 1881 1:2,500 OS map but there was no trace on site although a well head is still in place.

C   Staveley-in-Cartmel pound,
Grid ref: 338310,484930.
This structure is shown and
named as a pound on the 1892
1:2,500 OS map but the structure
only is shown on later maps.
Since then it has been roofed
with a door and window added.

It is on the lane leading to Cartmel from the A590 which was
greatly improved in the early 1970's. It is probable that the pound
was "improved" to be used as storage during this work as on closer
inspection it was found to contain several out of date road signs.

P   Stockdale Moor
(Kinniside) Mountain
pinfold.
Grid ref:
309078,509013.
This is an example of a
sheepfold on open moor
being used as a pinfold.
It is on the edge of
Stockdale Moor, now
stands only in outline
but it is possible to

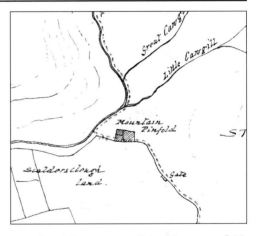

identify the three cells forming this Mountain or Moughton pinfold
so called because it was used to impound animals from the high
moor. Its purpose was similar to that of the usual pinfold in that it
was used to impound animals that were found on the moor during
the twice yearly drive in order to collect the pinding charge. This
rate was 12d for a work horse, 18d for a young horse, 12d for an
ox or cow and 2s6d for every 20 sheep. Stockdale Moor was an
extensive private agistment ground which provided summer grazing
for 1000 sheep and 100 horses from the coastal lands to the west of
the moor. The agistment or pinding was leased in the sixteenth and
seventeenth centuries from Lady Day, 20th April, to Harvest, 8th
September each year with the moor driven once or twice a year.

S   Strands pinfold, Millom. Grid ref: 318385,484228.
Shown on the 1867 1;10,560 OS map but today is marked by
two small standing stones. Local information indicated that was
demolished prior to 1930. It is noted on the Common Land
Register number 491.

NF   Sunderland pinfold. Not found.
A hand written manor court document dated 1361, held at
Cumbria Archives, states "Sunderland Pundfold is presented for
being out of repair". Its site could not be found.

C   Threapland pinfold, Aspatria. Grid ref: 315700,539300
This is an ancient hedged pinfold approximately 20mtrs square
with access at one corner. The hedge is growing on the top of a
small bank which was probably
originally strengthened by stones.
A modern gate has been placed at
the entrance and overall it is in
good condition with the interior
and surrounding area of grass well
kept. Because of its nature it is
unusual to find a hedged pinfold
still in existence. Its position in

the centre of the village at the entrance to a farm makes it a focal
point on what may be a village green. On the First Edition County
Series Ordnance Survey map of 1868 it is not named but is clearly
shown in outline. The centre of Threapland is shown as a semi-open
area around Threapland Hall.

NF   Threlkeld.
The site for this pinfold could not be traced although without
doubt there was a pinfold in Threlkeld. It is mentioned in the
history booklet in the church and in document PC/21/2-3 dated
1801 held in Carlisle Archives. The sheepfold shown to the south-
east of the village, on the edge of the fell before enclosure, is a
possible site shown on the 1862 OS map but not on the later 1899
one and no trace of the sheepfold can now be found.

S   Torpenhow pinfold, Aspatria. Grid ref: 320334,539704.
Pinfold shown at the side of the road next to the school on the 1867 1:2,500 OS map. The area now has modern housing on the site.

C   Troutbeck pinfold, Ambleside.
Grid ref: 340813,502746.
Although this structure has been suggested as a pinfold it is not named on any OS maps. It is next to High Fold Farm, is in the centre of the village and of a compatible size and

construction so possibly was the village pinfold. In the Troutbeck Village Guide published in 1999 Margaret Parsons recognises the use of this structure as a "fold" used for the protection of animals. It is currently used as a garden and there is no obvious natural water source so I will assume it is a pinfold until told otherwise!

P   Troutbeck – Town Head pinfold.
Grid ref: 341671,503928.
This pinfold is shown on the 1860 OS 1:2,500 map.
Although only the outline can be seen in the tumbled down walls of this pinfold it was once a significant pinfold in the life of the people of

the Troutbeck valley. It is located just off the coaching route to Kirkstone Pass and alongside the Ing Track coming in from the high fells to the fertile and highly prized grazing in the valley.

C   Ulverston pound.
Grid ref: 328563,478741
A small pinfold much altered from its original shape and size and was used as child's playground but now locked. It is shown on the Ulverston Town Plan map of 1890 and was Grade II listed in June 1972.

It was then described as "Possibly early C19 with later alterations. Mixed stone rubble. Roughly semi-circular on plan with straight side to the north and with walls approx. 1.5-2m high. The curved walls mostly have triangular copings. The straight wall steps upwards at its eastern end where a small building has been demolished. The entrance gateway, at the south-west side, has a stone lintel." It is believed to be the responsibility of South Lakeland District Council.

C   Warcop pinfold, Appleby-in-Westmorland.
Grid ref: 375002,515352
Clearly shown on the 1859 1:2,500
OS map but not named as a pinfold.
Prior to the rebuild there were only a
few stones on the site. The rebuild is by

Andy Goldsworthy, as part of the five year public art, landscape and environment commission, managed and developed by Cumbria County Council (1996-2002). It is one of a series of six "Cone pinfolds" where a stone cone has been constructed in the centre of the fold as a public artwork.

C   Watendlath. Grid ref: 327634,516352.
A reference held in Carlisle Archives
relates to the Manor of Borrowdale (D
LAW/1/176) dated 1875 stating that
John Cannon and Fletcher Wren had
fields including a "Green and pinfold".
This is likely to refer to the circular

structure named as a sheepfold on the 1867 OS 1:10,560 map. It is close to the hamlet of Watendlath beside a small beck feeding Watendlath Tarn.

R   Watermillock pound.
Grid ref:343124,523168
What remains of this pound may be
viewed from the bridge as it stands
on private land. There is one wall
left, but may be more remains in the
undergrowth. It was probably robbed

during road and bridge improvements. It is named on the 1864 1:2,500 OS map and although its current location seems unlikely for a pinfold there was probably a ford or lower level river crossing originally at this point. There are local plans for it to be preserved.

S Wigton pinfold. Grid ref: 325594,547841.

The original pinfold is shown on the 1864 1:500 Town Plan for Wigton at the junction of Low Moor Road and South End road, roads coming in from the moor. It was demolished probably in the 1950's when the junction was improved. The Evening Mail reported on 29th May 2009 that Anthony Gormley had at last rebuilt the pinfold as part of the arts project launched in 1996 – thirteen years after the main event.

C Winton pinfold.

Grid ref: 378800,510560.

A well maintained circular pinfold is to the eastern outskirts of Winton on the edge of Winton Common known as Hunger Rigg. It is shown on the 1859 1:2,500  OS map and registered on the Cumbria Sites and Monuments register number 1779.

S Workington pinfold. Grid ref: 300550,528330.

A square pinfold is shown on the 1867 OS 1:10,560 map and it stands in open pasture. The will of Mary Wilson (YDX473/1/2/1) dated 25th June 1805 held in Workington Archives leaves "various properties situate near the pinfold in Uppergate" to her daughter Catharine Wilson. Today it has been replaced by a row of Victorian terraced houses.

Glossary.

Agistment
When animals were driven to summer pastures and left with a herdsman. Payment was made per head to the owner of the pasture on which the animals grazed.

Ammercement
A fine imposed by the court for breach of a byelaw or order.

Bailiffe
A manor court official in charge of a manor.

Constable
A manor court official appointed to oversee other manor court officials.

Court Baron
A basic manorial court held by a lord for his tenants.

Court Leet
A manorial court to deal with a wider range of matters specifically minor criminal offences.

Estover
The right to take wood for necessary repairs or for fuel. Later widened to include the taking of bracken, heather and rushes for fuel and thatching.

Looker
An official appointed by the manor to oversee a particular aspect such as hedge looker, pinfold looker or house looker bringing any offenders to the court.

Paine
An order or byelaw imposed by the manor court.

Pasturage
The right to graze livestock on the common land.

Pinder
Manorial officer appointed to impound and look after livestock in the pound or pinfold.

Pinding	The right to impound stock and to charge for their grazing.
Pinfold or Pound	The structure or enclosure used to impound stray livestock.
Poundbreach	The repossessing, by breaking into the pound, of livestock already held there.
Poundloose	The money paid to the pinder to reclaim livestock from the pound.
Rescue	The repossessing, sometimes by force, livestock being driven to the pound.
Sheilings	Summer dwelling for shepherds on the high fells.
Stint	A numerical limit on the size of the right to graze on pasture.
Syke	A small stream or wet hollow area.
Township	A small community e.g. a village or hamlet.
Turbary	The collection or harvest of peat and stone.
Villein	A term used in the feudal era to denote a peasant (tenant farmer) who was legally tied to a lord of the manor.
Waste	Common or unimproved land.

Bibliography.

The Harvest of the Hills by Angus Winchester

Landscape and Society in Medieval Cumbria by Angus Winchester

Pounds or Pinfolds, and Lockups by B.M.Wilmott Dobbie

Webliography.

www.lancaster.ac.uk/fass/projects/manorialrecords

www.poundsandpinfolds.co.uk

www.english-heritage.org.uk/caring/listing/listed-buildings

www.sheepfoldscumbria.co.uk